RAZ

JENNIFER JULIE MILLER

<u>Jennifer Julie Miller</u>

*I want to dedicate this book and my entire career to my husband, **Rick.** There are no words to describe my love for you, but the one thing I really want to say is, thank you, for WANTING me, and for being my HERO!*

Also, I want to thank my parents, my amazing kids, and beautiful grandkids, my crazy aunt, and all my friends for your constant support. I especially thank my family for the hours on end you have had to listen to the insane ideas inside my head .... Even though most of you think I need to be evaluated!

ACKNOWLEDGMENTS

Cover Art by © Creative cover Designs (Vicki Adrian, Artist)
Beta Readers:
Lorene Palmer, Rick Miller, Ethel Nance.
Editor:
Lauren Meghoo
Photographs:
Shutterstock, Adobe
Inspirational imagination crew:
Jewel Shipley, Lauren Meghoo, Vicki Adrian.

Special thanks to Lauren; our daily talks make me feel like we have been friends forever. It's truly a blessing having you in my life! MISSSS Jewel, thank you for all your help and for keeping me young!

TRIGGER WARNINGS

Trigger Warnings

Please be aware that this book contains content that some readers may find disturbing. Recommended for mature readers only.

TO MY READERS

To all my new readers and loyal supporters, some of you reached out asking for a "Family Tree" for DaR. With only his father, Tyberius, and his 20-plus sons, I didn't think it would be much of a tree but more of a bush! So instead, I thought a summary would be best. Hope this works to keep everyone straight and if you've missed a book or only read a few, maybe this will bring you back to the series to read about all of DaR's 'boys' to date!!

SUMMARY OF THE
HOUSE OF DAR BOOKS.

DaR and Kira, Book One: DaR is the primary Commander over the Darverius solar system and father of twenty-two, now twenty-three sons and son of Elder Tyberius (book in the Forsaken series). Kira is the first human recovered in their region. She was abducted by the Korgons, held in cryostasis for eighty to hundred years and leaving behind her deceased husband, Rick, and two children, Marisa, and Cody. This book also introduces you to SAGE and Kira's pet Uana, Ickis.

XuL and Brittany, Book Two: As of this book, XuL is the oldest son of DaR, and he is also a general in DaR's regiment. A mix of his father and mother's species gives him very cruel features. Brittany is another human abducted by the Korgons and sold at a livestock market along with Kira. She is bought by a scientist and held in a floating fortress and tended to by an AI named, DREAM. XuL saves her and they have their first grandchild, Keida. You also meet the Selin SeeSee and Brits's pet Uana, Iggy. Other characters in this book are the Priestess Zlana; her daughter Zura, who is the warrior princess that will later take over the battle training duties of Keida. Zura is also featured in ZoD and gets her own book in OrO.

SoL and Alana, Book Three: Second oldest son of DaR, his goal is to be the favorite 'Unka' to Keida. Towering over all DaR's other sons, he also has the biggest heart. He rescues Alana under false pretenses before they're both captured by the Banhan. The couple end up running the battle cruiser, Falcor together.

RaZ and Katherine, Book Four: RaZ in the third oldest son and is DaR's most talented pilot and assassin. The only son with wings, he also must have blood to live on. He mounts a rescue mission to Earth to save his mate Katherine, and his grandfather, Tyberius (from my book "Forgotten"). You also meet Victoria, Emma, and Lucas (of the Forsaken series) and Hellhounds: Raven, Ghost, Glory, and Thorn. First mention of Danny.

Tordan and Luna, Book Five: He's DaR's best friend and helped raise all his sons, so they consider him a second father. He's also second in command of Falcor and has cybernetic parts. Luna was found in Targres Four in the scientific sector and most of her body has become cyborg. Reassembled by the AI, ENAC; he was trying to perfect the perfect host. You are also introduced to AMI, the AI medic unit. Hugo is a huge part of this story.

Hugo and Miya, Book Six: Hugo is the red Phlox alien with black horns that tried to steal Kira from the market in book one and DaR killed him. He is part cyborg and has very limited memories of his origins. Miya's dad stole a pod and launched her into space just hours before Earth collapsed. Hugo receives her from the Jynrel pirates in really bad shape. This book also features Tyberius, as well as SAGE, SCOUT, and AMI. Also, you learn about alien coffee.

AvX and Ivy, Book Eight: Ivy runs away from home and gets kidnapped by the Korgon, and later sold to a brothel. This is the first book where the Waldrin are spoken about. AvX is on a mission to find the perfect present for Keida because he and SoL are always competing for the favorite 'Unka' status. He finds Ivy in a cage being guarded by an Owl Alterra and rescues her.

ViN and Ember, Book Ten: Ember is the second female found in a pod, but it hits the surface of Targres Four so hard, it goes underground. Being the best tracker of DaR's sons, we find ViN, going out into the desolate area to search for her. He finds her just as she is being sacrificed to the Lava God. She can't understand him, but his translator is working fine so he has to gain her trust as they make their way back to the surface.

SiN and Jade, Book Twelve SiN has been lied to his entire life, and it's warped him, so he has dedicated himself to ruining his father, DaR. He gets hurt in ViN's book and comes back to Darverius to seek sanctuary in Mystic, the oldest guardian Tree of Life. This is where he meets his violet-eyed 'Angel', Jade. He is actually the oldest son of DaR. This book is quite an adventure.

ZoD and Tessa, Book Thirteen: ZoD is the second commander in the Darverius sector, and his people keep coming up missing due to the Waldrin, a race he doesn't know how to defeat. He has a secret lab in the outer sector where he has been performing test on multiple females. Trying to figure out which species' blood is poisonous to the Waldrin. This is where Tessa is taken, and the moment he smells her, he knows she is his. You also meet his children, Raya, Onyx, Elexa, Zllera, and Wynd. Zura and Raya fight together in this book. This is also the first time the Warrior Trials are mentioned. Others in this book include: DaR, Kira, Tordan, Luna, Alana, SoL, Zura, SiN, Jade.

OrO and Zura, Book Fifteen: He is a guard at the palace, and she has secretly loved him all her life, but her mate bond never formed. Zura is a warrior who her people look up to, and he is a soft-hearted, yet stern male that the children all love. You meet her wicked mother, Zlana, as well as Rosad, Kraga, and Azog. This is the first appearance of MeK, another of DaR's sons and the pod engineer.

EvO and Qwin, Book Sixteen: Captain of the Destroyer, EvO is sent out with ViN, LeX, and Rafe, along with an entire crew to find the missing pods that escaped Earth before it was destroyed. He finds Qwin and must save her from a malfunctioning pod. She was forced inside the pod and has extreme survivor's guilt. Their story continues in LeX and in the (pirate series - The Brigands of Ruk: Falon). We're introduced to the humans, James, and Carla as well as Lacie and Ricky.

Lex and Rylie, Book Seventeen: The main medic of the Destroyer LeX is sent out with his brothers to find the missing pods. He finds Rylie in a pod that he has to practically tear apart to keep her from dying within. Only for her to end up being in a coma, where the only way he can communicate with her is in his dreams. This book also covers Rafe and Cassandra's story and how they fall in love, as well as Ember and ViN and their new little dragon, Ami Lynn.

MeK and Lacie, Book Eighteen: MeK is the primary engineer for all specialized equipment, including the housing pods and the healing chambers. He's assigned to Ethra to help build the future home for the humans retrieved from the Nebula. He is brainwashed by his mother and fights the pull and attraction he has for Lacie. Lacie is a young klutz who seems to fall into one problem after another. This book even has its own serial killer. You are introduced to Briar and BuK, as well as a load of other side characters like James and Carla, Vedece, and KyT. Ohhh, and don't forget little KIKI, our baby Suet.

BuK and Briar, Book Nineteen: BuK is my little soft-hearted sweetheart who thinks that the world makes love way too hard. Boy likes girl, and she likes him back ... problem solved. But when push comes to shove, and the world tries to take the girl he loves from him, you see a whole other side of him, as he will give all to save her. Briar is loud and fun and loves to push everyone's buttons, but since landing on Ethra, she has decided Pink is now her favorite color. Just how do you get someone as shy as BuK to act on his feelings? You play strip poker and hope for the best. You meet HaL in this book as well.

KyT and Vedece, Book Twenty: KyT is my talking, walking tree who is fascinated with all things human, but especially Vedece who does no wrong in his eyes. She keeps him at arm's length throughout the previous books, but he is patient, and it pays off when he gets the girl. This book also contains Ricky and Ginger's HEA and ties in the Brigands of Ruk series with Falon being adopted into the DaR's family as one of his sons.

For those of you who were really paying attention to the list above or were looking at the List on Amazon, no, I have not forgotten how to count or make a numerical list (hahaha), but there were a few novellas I wrote as follows:

Between RaZ & Tordan is "A House of DaR Celebration"

Between AvX & ViN is "SAGE"

Between ViN & SiN is "SCOUT"

Between ZoD & OrO is "A House of DaR Vacation"

All will be available on audio by the end of 2027.

CHAPTER 1

RAZ

I hug each of my brothers firmly and try to make light of what is coming, that is, until I get to Father. I struggle like a youngling, fighting back the tears when his strong arms wrap around me tightly. After a moment, I push away from him and force myself to walk up the ramp. I cannot say another word or I am going to fall apart right here. I turn back, looking at each of them and saving this scene in my head to pull strength from in the future and the numerous years ahead that I will be alone. Standing on the ramp of the Traveler as the door closes is one of the hardest things I have ever done. Red tears flow down my face as I watch Father struggle with letting me go. I will never forget the look on his face when he told me, I am *not willing to lose a son just to save my father*. It is hard to contemplate that this may be the very last time I ever lay eyes on my father or any of my brothers. If I succeed, it will be a glorious day. If I fail ... well then, I will have let everyone down.

· · ·

IF I AM HONEST, I DO NOT KNOW HOW MUCH ARGUING I WOULD have done to be the one being sent on this mission if it had not been for Katherine. I have been on hundreds of assignments, but none of them have been as important to me as this one.

THE MOMENT THAT TRANSMISSION CAME THROUGH AND I LAID eyes on her ... my whole world shifted. I went from being the family jokester to a male on a mission. The whys, where's, or even how's have racked my brain ever since. It is truly amazing how fate ties certain lives together.

THIS BEGAN WHEN FATE FIRST TWISTED MY FAMILY INTO ITS plans for tomorrow when my grandfather, Tyberius, left Darverius on a routine council mission. He boarded a space cruiser and simply disappeared. Grandfather and six of our elders ... gone...not a single trace of them anywhere.

My father, DaR, being his only son never stopped searching. I asked him one time when I was a youngling, why he was still looking for him? Father told me he knew in his heart that his father was alive somewhere and then he asked me, *how long would I look if it was him?*

I REMEMBER STANDING UP AS TALL AS I COULD, WHICH WAS ONLY about to his waist at the time and telling him, *'I would never stop!'*

HE KNELT DOWN AND PULLED ME INTO A HUGE HUG, THEN whispered, *"Now you understand! Remember son, we never forsake or forget the ones we love because in the end, their love is all the Lord of the Light will allow us to take with us when we leave this world."*

Like always though, life continued to move forward and many rotations later my own father, due to the duties and responsibilities of his military position had twenty-two sons of his own. All of us are unique, with different abilities shaped by our individual mothers and their diverse heritages. During this time, father temporarily suspended much of his searching and devoted himself to raising his boys and protecting our home world, Darverius, instilling in each of us the importance of family and honor.

The next time fate stepped in was after we were all grown and father had moved on from the family home and finally acquired the beloved mountaintop he had always coveted. Shortly after his dwelling was finished, he unwillingly purchased a housemate ... a tiny human female that had been kidnapped, brutalized, and was on the brink of death. Her world had been destroyed and everything she loved had been ripped from her arms. But once again, fate was not done playing with our lives, because if she had not been torn away from everything she knew and loved, she would never have been in that slave market, and Father would not have found his mate. She quickly became the one thing my father simply could not live without. He would and will do anything to make her happy.

Right after she came into father's life, my brother SoL started searching for answers. Where did she come from? How long had she been gone? Are there others of her kind out there? Father was doing anything he could to provide some sort of information to ease her mind as she struggled with the idea of never going home again and the loss of her human mate.

UNFORTUNATELY, BECAUSE OF HER RARITY, FATHER'S HOUSEMATE, Kira became an obsession for some of the species in our galaxy, and the hunt for more of her kind began across the galaxy. After a failed abduction attempt, father refused to leave her alone unless one of his sons was always with her. All my father's sons are a little *over the top,* Kira's words not mine, and the first meeting she had with us... well, it seemed to go quite poorly!

I LAUGH TO MYSELF WHEN I REMEMBER THE MOMENT KIRA LAID eyes on me for the first time, and how terrified she was. She screamed out a name that would change my life...VAMPIRE! After she calmed down, I had no idea that one word, or the simple conversation that followed, would have us all looking for her world with new urgency. She told us about the legends on her planet that she called *folklore, and* then she randomly gave us six of the seven elders, including my own grandfather's name. My father, DaR, threw every resource we had into finding Earth after that, and then the most amazing thing happened. We didn't only find her world, but we also found grandfather and ... my Katherine.

IF KIRA HAD NEVER BEEN ABDUCTED, FATHER NEVER WOULD HAVE found my grandfather, and I would have never found my beloved. How many more moves in this game of life had to be altered for us to be right here, right now?

. . .

MY MIND DRIFTS AS I WATCH THE STARS' LIGHTS PASS BY. I HAVE nothing but time to think about the things that have led up to this moment; all the how's and why's. Am I just another piece of thread in this cosmic blanket of interwoven fates?

A BEEPING NOISE BRINGS ME OUT OF MY THOUGHTS AS THE Traveler alerts me that we are approaching the first jump. SoL has designed a marvelous craft in the Traveler. She has all the luxuries of home and the flying capabilities of a stealth fighter. Currently, she is performing above our expectations. When I first came aboard, Traveler's AI was only used to taking all orders from SoL. That has caused a few mistakes, such as us almost hitting a stray asteroid, but Traveler is finally starting to listen to me, although it is still unsure whether it wants to obey.

I STRAP IN AND WATCH THE INSTRUMENT PANEL AS THE JUMP coordinates quickly approach. None of us has ever done this type of "jump" space traveling, so this will be a new experience all around.

"RAZ, THE JUMP WILL COMMENCE IN MOMENTS!"

TORDAN'S VOICE COMES OVER THE SPEAKER AS HE IS MONITORING the Traveler from the Explorer right now. Even though Tordan is currently on a mission with XuL, he has still spent as much time as possible discussing the potential problems I may have as he flies XuL, and his own sick little human, toward Xulas. My mind wanders for a moment with all the things happening at home. I feel like I have already been gone forever, my life crawling by out here in space. It seems like I am missing crucial events, and they are all living their lives without me, especially XuL, as his is in chaos.

WHEN I HADN'T HEARD FROM XuL FOR ROTATIONS, I ASKED SoL where our big brother had run off to. Apparently, another conversation between XuL and Kira this time, sent XuL out on a mission to find the other human female that had been captured along with Kira. Tordan has not been able to tell me much about what happened because he is scared to talk in front of XuL. It seems that this female only has rotations left to live due to the condition she was found in and XuL is blaming himself for not getting to her quicker. My heart hurts for my brother as I saw the pain in his eyes the few times he stepped away from her to talk to me. I can tell he has quickly become attached to this female. I only hope she can see the honorable male he is, as most do not see past his fearsome appearance. Another beep jerks me out of my daydreaming.

"THE TRAVELER HAS ALREADY ALERTED ME, TORDAN. LET US hope this new program of SoL's works! I would be lying if I said I was not a little nervous out here."

THE SCREEN IN FRONT OF ME LIGHTS UP AND MY FATHER'S FACE appears. "RaZ, we have run hundreds of simulations on our end, and everything looks fine. SoL has informed me that you will feel slightly disoriented, but that it will pass quickly. We believe we will be able to trace you fully through the first jump. Know that I will come for you if things go astray! May the Lord of Light hold you safely in his grasp, Son."

. . .

"I will prevail, Father. All your offspring know you would never forsake us."

He nods and simply stands there, watching me until the feed goes black. I am a trained assassin and one of the deadliest males in our solar system,' but honestly, I am scared. I have never been on a single mission where I did not know every step I needed to take to be successful. My brother XuL is a master of battle strategies, and between the two of us, we looked at every angle, never sending our men or ourselves into battle unprepared ... until now.

I hear *three, two, one,* and the whole ship shakes slightly. A flash of bright light makes me turn my head and close my eyes. I feel like my skin is being pulled tight for a mere tic, and then everything settles down. I shake my head and stretch my wings out, my whole body giving a shiver,

"RaZ, can you hear me?"

"Loud and clear, SoL."

I shake my head. "That was strange. I would not say that it was painful, or even uncomfortable, just unexpected more than anything else." SoL's face appears on the screen. I can see his massive fingers typing in commands as he talks to me and the ship at the same time.

"TRAVELER, UPDATE ON YOUR STATUS?"

"MASTER SoL, I HAVE SENT A REPAIR BOT TO READJUST A PANEL on the back thruster; just a minor repair. All other programs are operating at optimum performance."

"Send all coordinates from this point on to Falcor so we may chart your return path."

"CONFIRMED, MASTER SoL."

SoL RELAXES AFTER THE SHIP RESPONDS AND LOOKS UP AT ME. "Well big brother, at least the first jump was a success. Now just two more to go. Are you getting space travel restlessness yet?"

"I AM TRYING NOT TO THINK ABOUT IT, BUT THERE ARE MOMENTS when I feel like the walls are closing in on me. I am used to being in the air most of the time, so I do not know how you stand all this walking." I hear all of them laughing at me in the background. "I think I will head to the cargo bay later to stretch my wings out, and I am going to recheck the maps again. If all is clear, I believe I will put myself into a light sleep for a few lunar rotations." I see one of the personnel walk up behind him, trying to get his attention. "Go on SoL, comm back when you get a chance. I am not going anywhere."

He nods, and the screen goes black.

They have spent many a rising talking to me, keeping me company through the long hours in space. Normally, I would have a full crew with me, so I had the noise and companionship of others, but now everything is quiet. I have never been on a stealth mission until now, and I am not sure I have the personality to be alone. I would be lying if I did not admit to being a little lonely.

I yearn for Katherine, a female I have never met in person, touched or even had the pleasure of hearing her voice for more than a moment. The fact is, I feel like my very soul is being pulled in her direction. It is unsettling, this all-consuming need to be with her, a perfect stranger. I only saw her for a matter of moments, but that was long enough for me to memorize her every feature.

I believe I am a little over halfway to Earth from the calculations we were able to decipher from the information ANDI sent. I keep sending out random signals, hoping one of them will get through the closer I get, but nothing yet. There has been no further contact from grandfather or ANDI.

. . .

I unstrap myself and head toward the cargo bay. There is not enough room for me to fly in there, but I can at least stretch my wings out. After I am done, I think I will grab a bag of life elixir and take a nap; maybe a couple risings nap actually, if the coordinates seem clear around me.

After the third jump, I will lose all contact with SoL, Tordan, and my father. This is the part of the trip I am least looking forward to. I will also be out of range from the communication systems on Darverius. Father is trying to retrofit a space station in the outer quadrant for message relay, but it won't be functioning quickly enough to help me now. Hopefully, it will be up and running by the time I make it back on my return trip to the third jump's coordinates.

The plan is for me to put myself into a deep sleep for at least a whole orbital rotation once we clear our galaxy. I have decided to ration the blood packets I brought with me in case the third jump goes wrong, and I cannot put myself into a deep slumber.

The Traveler has been equipped with an alarm system that will wake me quickly if need be, but as finicky as she is about taking orders from me, who knows what she will deem a risk?

Within steps of being inside the large cargo hold, I extend my wings. They flutter as they stretch out around me. They are beginning to feel stiff from nonuse. I flap them, lifting myself a few inches off the ground. I shut my eyes and dream of my beloved home in the dark forest. If I think hard enough, I can almost smell its scents around me. For a moment, I see Katherine standing in a field of flowers, her long black hair streaming out behind her. She looks troubled and deep in thought, then the sound of a child's laughter jerks my eyes open.

I shake my head as I float back to the floor. My mind is playing tricks on me. It's time for food and a long nap.

CHAPTER 2
RAZ

I grab a bag of blood out of the warmer and head toward the back of the ship. "Traveler, I will be in a light sleep for several rotations, and you are to notify me of any potential problems immediately. Are those orders clear?"

"Confirmed, Captain RaZ. I have all sensors set on high alert."

The captain's suite is pure luxury and almost larger than my own private quarters at home. I did have the bed reconfigured before this flight for my wings as it is easier for me to lie down on my stomach for long periods of time. My wings are so large now that they get sore if I lay on them for long.

I tilt the bag back and empty the contents in seconds. My body hungers for more and I almost return to the makeshift kitchen, but I refuse to give in. The last thing I need is to accidentally shut down right before I land on Earth. I can tolerate some hard foods, but only in small quantities. However, the bed looks inviting and I know sleep will help with the cravings.

Undressing, I flop down on the bed, tucking my head into the small indentation in the mattress. My wings stretch out over me, hanging freely off the edge. It does not take long for my mind to calm, and unconsciously, I reach out for Katherine as sleep envelopes me.

The sound of laughter has me looking around at a place I have never seen before. I step forward and feel my feet sink into the soft ground below me; everything smells strange. Large mammals stick their heads out of what look like holding pens of some sort. As I walk forward, I barely move out of the way in time as a small female races past me. Long black hair streams out behind her as she darts toward this dwelling's opening. I have no idea why, but I immediately turn to follow her. Her laughter pulls at my very soul. I start running when I lose sight of her through the doorway. As I clear the entrance, the light immediately makes me back up into the darkness. But the urge to follow her is stronger than the pain of the bright light. Stepping out hesitantly, I shade my eyes from the powerful sun above me. The sun's light has never bothered me before, but I can feel my skin burning now.

I am shocked further as I look around at the primitive buildings. I start to walk forward when I hear small footsteps running back to me again. It is the same female, but this time she has another with her. This one has light-colored hair and seems frail compared to the other female. They are both beautiful to be so young, but their auras are quite different. Neither of them can be over a few spans old. I have never seen the clothing they have on before; long, thick, flowing material hangs clear to their feet. I watch the one with light-colored hair hike the material up, trying to keep it off the dirty ground around her as she runs laughing with the other female. They come straight at me ... like they can't see me standing here. I step out of their way just moments before they run back into the dark building behind me.

"Come on Emma, you have to see them, they are all so beautiful."

"I'm coming, Kat, but I can't get this dress dirty, or you know I will get in trouble."

"I'll tell mother it was my fault."

I watch as they both disappear into the last holding cell together. I walk behind them cautiously, wondering why they never noticed me standing practically in front of them. I am sort of hard to miss with these wings. I can hear the girls cooing over something and then the whine of a small animal.

I look over the top of the holding cell, shocked to see them sitting in the middle of the mammal's food, playing with what looks like baby Selins with no teeth. They are all different colors, and the females take turns hugging and playing with each of them.

I see the black-haired female take something out of her pocket.

It must be food of some sort because all but one of the little animals pounce on her playfully, wanting a bite. The other female, I notice, seems to have become attached to a solid black one with a white-tipped ear. The dark-haired one starts to reach for it, and it bites her hand. Immediately, blood pools up on her small hand. I force myself to look away from the blood, and that is when I notice the small animal is different from the others.

He may appear the same, but there is a dark, fiery essence all around this animal. The girl who has been holding him the whole time scolds him gently, and as she starts to turn him around in her arms, I watch one of his long claws scratch the inside of her wrist.

She whispers to him, "Oww, Blacky, you must be gentle, honey. I will get you a snack and bring it back this evening."

"Let me see, did he hurt you too, Emma? Boys are always so rough. I'm gonna ask mom if I can keep this one! Don't you think his coloring looks like a ghost?"

"Oh, my ... look at the blood on your hand. Did he hurt you bad, Kat?"

"Nahh, just shocked me more than anything. Come on, let's get them settled down and go in for dinner. I will sneak down to the kitchen afterward and get some food. When I go to my lessons, you can sneak it out here to them."

I watch the girls silently as they tuck what they are calling 'pups' back into the corner of this holding cell. As they approach the door, I step back out of the way and they walk past me like I am not even standing here. I start to call out, but I do not want to startle them. I was a youngling once too, but I would have noticed a stranger with wings hovering over me.

As for that matter, where am I and who are these two young ones? What was I doing? I was on a trip somewhere, something important!

I jerk in my sleep and push myself straight up in the bed, my mind fuzzy and disoriented.

"Captain RaZ, Commander DaR has been trying to comm you. Now that you have awakened, would you like me to patch him through?"

"Yes, that is fine."

I watch my father's worried face appear on a holo screen on the wall. "Frack RaZ, you had all of us worried! I have been trying to reach you for several rotations now. Are you unwell?"

"No, I do not think so, but ... something happened. How long have I been out?"

"According to Traveler, you have been in a deep sleep for twenty lunar rotations. Tordan began to worry when he had not heard anything from you and contacted me. Damnit son, I tried every-thing! You know to always keep your personal communicator on you and I was only a rotation away from coming after you." I watch him pacing in front of the holo screen. "I should never have allowed you to go on this mission alone. I am torn right now because two of my beloved sons are headed in opposite directions on dangerous missions. I am going to have a full head of gray hair before my time due to all of you. I probably should have thought that through before the lottery gave me so many of you!"

He growls when I laugh. "I apologize, Father, I did not mean to sleep that long, but it was like I was somewhere else. I believe I was dreaming, although it seemed almost like a memory, just not mine. How would that be possible?"

"I will have SoL run some diagnostics. Maybe it is a side effect of being in space for so long or caused by the jump."

"It all felt so real to me ... I know I have a highly active imagination, but I have no way to describe the things I saw. I could even hear the sounds and the smells all around me. You would have thought I was actually there, watching."

Father pulls up a chair and runs his hands through his hair. "You did not recognize anything?"

"Not at all, but there was a youngling. A dark-haired female I had the strangest urge to follow. The oddest part was that in the dream, their sun was able to hurt my skin."

"Does your female not have black hair?"

"Yes, but she is far from being a child; these were younglings."

"Tordan, are you linked in right now?"

"Yes, I am 'here."

"Have you ever heard of anything like this?"

"I believe I have read it in a passage somewhere, but only because Tyberius was translating the text at the time. But I do not know enough about it to tell you anything accurately. RaZ, I will have Falcor link up with SCOUT and see if he can find anything in the scrolls. I honestly think your spirit is seeking out your female. If this happens again, try to study your surroundings. Maybe this will help you locate her when you get closer."

Father turns back to me with a huge smile on his face. "Oh, by the way, you are getting ready to be an 'Uncle,' or that is what Kira calls it anyway."

"What the frack? I have not been asleep that long, have I?"

"You know you boys do nothing by half measures. XuL's female Brittany is pregnant. I will let him give you all the details, as her pregnancy is progressing quickly. Because all of you were conceived and born on different planets, I was never present during any of your mothers' pregnancies. I did not realize until now how much I missed out on with each of you. This whole miracle of creation is fascinating, especially watching her turn green. Now that things have calmed down a little for XuL, I will make sure he contacts you soon."

"I do not know what to think. My big brother is going to be a father and I will be an uncle. Frack! The little one will not even know me. I will just be a random name and that angers me to no end. I should be the primary one to spoil our first little youngling!"

CHAPTER 3
RAZ

I look out the viewer at the nothingness surrounding me. I feel like I am running in place, my insides are jittery, and I feel anxious. There are even times when I swear I smell perfume in the air. I have even glimpsed someone standing beside me a few times. I feel like I am being haunted.

"Traveler, how long do we have until the second jump?"

"Captain RaZ, at our current speed, it will commence in forty rotations."

I lay my head down on the console in front of me, trying to ignore the flashing lights. I know if the Traveler could shake her head, she would because I have asked her ten times this rising about the distance we still have to go. At this rate, I do not know if I will make it to Earth with my mind still intact. The loneliness is truly getting to me. I did not realize how bad it was until I was listening to XuL talk about his mate last darkness. I have never seen him so at ease in his own skin. His little female has done wonders for his self-esteem.

I FEEL BAD NOW BECAUSE I KNOW I WAS UNABLE TO HIDE THE shock on my face from XuL when she suddenly walked in and pulled him down for a quick kiss. I mean, it is one thing to be told about their love and another to see it firsthand. I had to make myself close my mouth when she turned toward the holo screen, waving at me before saying, "RaZ, don't keep him too long, I need my snuggles."

APPARENTLY, I WAS THE ONLY ONE FEELING UNCOMFORTABLE with their intimacy, as she talked to me like she had been around me her whole life. Even though she was not in front of the screen for long, I could still see her arms and neck were pale green in color. How utterly fascinating, and I am missing all of it.

MY MIND DRIFTS OFF AS I FANTASIZE ABOUT MINE AND Katherine's first kiss and the possibility of younglings of my own one day.

I pull my cloak up over my head as the cold rain beats down on my back. The powerful storm pulls at my wings as I hover outside a clear opening that looks inside a darkened room which smells of sickness and death.

. . .

MOVEMENT ON THE BED CATCHES MY ATTENTION AS I BRUSH THE water off my face. I float closer to the opening, only to see multiple people rushing around a small figure lying on a bed of some sort. I can smell the poison racing through her small frame as she lays there, shivering and moaning out in pain.

HER LONG BLACK HAIR LAYS LIMPLY AROUND HER SWEAT-SLICKENED face. She calls out a name, 'Emma'. Then she mumbles, 'Mommy, don't let them hurt her, promise me!' I can tell the woman sitting on the bed is her mother by the way she tenderly rubs her face. The woman tries to calm the child, but she continues to call out for this 'Emma' to the point that she is getting more upset the longer she calls out the name.

THE MOTHER PUSHES A STERN-LOOKING MALE OUT OF HER WAY, AND I see her kneel almost to the floor. When she turns back to where I can see her, she is carrying the small, light-haired girl in her arms. She too seems extremely sick and the older lady is having a hard time holding her she is trembling so badly. She tucks the two girls in together and the dark-haired one immediately calms down.

I CAN TELL THE OLDER MAN IS FURIOUS, BUT THE MOTHER POINTS AT the door for him to leave. While the parents are fighting, I watch the girls on the bed. The small, dark-haired one grasps her friend's hand tightly. I watch in complete horror as her little body shivers and she gasps, taking her last breath.

I FEEL LIKE MY OWN HEART IS BREAKING AS I WATCH HELPLESSLY. I try to pound on the opening, but my hand passes right through it. Nothing I *do gets their attention. The mother turns back toward the bed and lets out a pained scream that will haunt me forever. She knew her daughter was gone before she ever touched her cooling body.*

I START TO BACK AWAY FROM THE PAINFUL SCENE, WONDERING WHY I am seeing this small youngling's life pass as I have no knowledge of who she is. Then something cold touches the side of my face. Startled, I turn, only to find inches separating me from the dark hollow eyes of the young one floating beside me.

Her eyes flash red and I can feel her anger surround us as she sees how they are now treating the other girl, who is still fighting for her very life. I watch as the dark-haired one's spirit flies to the girl's defense, but to no avail.

IN THE BLINK OF AN EYE, I FIND MYSELF SOMEWHERE ELSE. I AM IN A crowd of people standing around a deep hole in the ground. The grief and suffering take my breath as the ground in this area seems to be saturated with it.

I LOOK UP AT THE MASSIVE STONE, MARKING WHAT I BELIEVE IS A grave and my heart hits my throat. I have no idea how I know what it says, but I feel like the words are now carved into my very soul. 'Here lies our beloved daughter, **Katherine Elizabeth Ione.**

I COLLAPSE TO MY KNEES. NO... NO... SHE IS ALIVE. I SAW HER! WHAT is happening and what am I seeing? A giggle catches my attention, and I feel my anger spike. Who would dare behave this way at a time like this?

. . .

A GROWL LEAVES MY THROAT AS I TURN TOWARD THE NOISE, AND standing only inches from me once again is the dark-haired child, a small, pale pup playing at her feet. But there is something wrong with her; she is not solid. She appears to be floating in a fog of sorts, her features changing constantly from younger to older. The word ghost *flickers through my mind. This dark-haired female has been my Katherine all along. She seems to notice me for the first time, and I almost jerk away when her small hand grazes my cheek.*

I FEEL LIKE SOMEONE HAS SPED THROUGH MY WHOLE LIFE, OR MAYBE it is her life passing by in seconds while she touches me. I watch it all from her eyes as the little light-haired girl grows into a woman. Her Emma, as she calls her, is beaten and hurt over and over. I can feel Katherine's frustrations and helplessness at not being able to help her friend from the grave.

THEN TIME SLOWS FOR A SECOND. EMMA IS RUNNING FROM something and I watch as a man appears out of the dark. He saves her, but he is different ... though almost familiar in appearance. I watch Katherine float through walls and walk upon the unfamiliar ground as she watches his every move to see if he is worthy of her dearest friend. Things start to flash before my eyes so quickly that I cannot see them clearly anymore. There is a huge black ... Hellhound? Rage, they call him ... and then there is a fire and people everywhere are dying.

THEN I SEE EMMA. SHE IS IN A DEEP SLEEP AND HER BODY IS changing in a manner that will never allow her to be hurt physically again. Somehow the man has changed her and she is finally safe now. But I do not understand how as all of this is happening so quickly in front of me. The male is lying with Emma in a dark room, watching over her way below the ground as her body becomes something else. His love for this timid female can be felt throughout the dwelling they are residing under.

Untrusting in the weakness of this new love, Katherine *paralyzes the male momentarily as she approaches him from above.* **'Love her for eternity, or I'll be back to collect what's mine.'** These words stick in my head.

I do not know how much time goes by, but then there is a *bright light and the sound of a young one crying. I am in another unknown place, but this time I am here alone. I cannot sense Katherine watching with me from anywhere. I seem to be looking down at what appears to be a birth, and I gasp. I know the moment the child takes her first breath ... because I just took my first real one too.*

I have no idea how or why I have seen any of this, but my *Katherine was just reborn. Her parents are none other than the young girl she has been protecting this entire time ... her Emma. The man comes from the shadows and for some reason, I feel like I need to know who this man is. But no matter what I do, I cannot see his face clearly, but his features and the way he moves remind me of someone.*

The scene fades as my private communicator buzzes on my arm, *"RaZZZZZZZZ!"*

. . .

I HEAR THE TRAVELER YELLING OUT MY NAME SECONDS BEFORE I am almost knocked out of my chair and just catch myself before being thrown to the floor.

"TRAVELER, REPORT STATUS!"

"CAPTAIN, WE HAVE ENTERED AN UNKNOWN ASTEROID FIELD. I did not detect it on my scanners until we were already surrounded. I have been implementing evasive maneuvers, but one of the energy panels was clipped and I got distracted trying to pull the sail in and did not maneuver quickly enough to avoid a collision with a smaller object. I sent the repair bots out to cover the opening immediately, but I am afraid we may have lost one of the battery packs. The second jump coordinates will be upon us before I can override the sequence."

"SLOW DOWN OUR DIRECT SPEED AND GIVE YOURSELF TIME TO mend the outer hull and then quarantine the damaged battery until we get into a stable flight pattern."

THE TRAVELER STARTS TO ANSWER ME WHEN SUDDENLY THE whole control panel goes dark. The ship comes to a complete stop like we suddenly hit an invisible wall.

I GRAB AN OXYGEN MASK AS I SEE ONE OF THE OUTER WALLS start to ice up. Before I have time to panic, I hear a loud beep and then the entire ship reboots. I throw the mask down.

. . .

"Wʜᴀᴛ ᴛʜᴇ ꜰʀᴀᴄᴋ ᴊᴜꜱᴛ ʜᴀᴘᴘᴇɴᴇᴅ, Tʀᴀᴠᴇʟᴇʀ?"

"Cᴀᴘᴛᴀɪɴ, ᴄᴀɴ ʏᴏᴜ ᴘʟᴇᴀꜱᴇ ꜱᴄᴀɴ ʏᴏᴜʀ ᴄʀᴇᴅᴇɴᴛɪᴀʟꜱ? Currently, you are not authorized to access that information."

"Tʀᴀᴠᴇʟᴇʀ, ᴡᴇ ʀᴇᴀʟʟʏ ɴᴇᴇᴅ ᴛᴏ ᴡᴏʀᴋ ᴏɴ ʏᴏᴜʀ ꜱᴇɴꜱᴇ ᴏꜰ ʜᴜᴍᴏʀ ... can you still contact Falcor?"

"Aꜰꜰɪʀᴍᴀᴛɪᴠᴇ."

Iᴛ ᴛᴀᴋᴇꜱ ᴍᴇ ᴀ ᴛɪᴄ ᴛᴏ ᴏᴠᴇʀʀɪᴅᴇ ʜᴇʀ ᴄᴏᴅᴇꜱ, ʙᴜᴛ I ꜰɪɴᴀʟʟʏ ɢᴇᴛ ᴀ direct link to Falcor.

"Tᴏʀᴅᴀɴ, SᴏL, ᴄᴀɴ ʏᴏᴜ ʙᴏᴛʜ ʜᴇᴀʀ ᴍᴇ?"

I see Tordan's face for a moment on screen.

"I ᴀᴍ ʜᴇʀᴇ RᴀZ; ᴡᴇ ꜱᴇᴇᴍᴇᴅ ᴛᴏ ʜᴀᴠᴇ ʟᴏꜱᴛ ʏᴏᴜ ꜰᴏʀ ᴀ ʟɪᴛᴛʟᴇ ʙɪᴛ there."

"Tᴏʀᴅᴀɴ, ᴛʜɪꜱ ʙᴜᴄᴋᴇᴛ ᴏꜰ ʙᴏʟᴛꜱ ꜱᴇᴇᴍꜱ ᴛᴏ ʜᴀᴠᴇ ʀᴇꜱᴇᴛ ʜᴇʀꜱᴇʟꜰ. I hope my brother is close because she will not listen to a single command I give her!"

. . .

Before he can say a single word to me the whole ship starts to shake, and the comm link goes silent. Apparently, the second jump was closer than I imagined, and now the ship is running automatically; simply engaged once the coordinates were reached.

I grasp onto the chair arms, gritting my teeth as it feels like my bones are being rattled inside my body. I say a prayer the moment the ship starts to calm. I try to pull up the ship's condition and reconnect to Tordan, but every command I input comes back unauthorized.

In a last attempt to contact Falcor, I hit my personal communicator. The moment it dings, SoL's face appears on screen, and I swear I almost weep in relief.

"SoL, thank the Lord of Light you can still answer me. Look, your girl here is refusing to take any orders from me, and I could use some help. We sustained some damage and she rebooted herself. I need you to send me the override codes in case this happens again."

I hear him say, "Traveler, report damage and coordinates."

. . .

I cannot tell if she has answered him or not, because the sound and the picture blink in and out. I am catching bits and pieces of SoL telling Traveler to slow down and that the third jump coordinates are coming up too fast. I receive a hidden message from Tordan containing the codes and what appears to be the ship's schematics via a personal link that the Traveler cannot access.

SoL's voice comes in faintly, "RaZ you must find a way to slow her down. You are heading into uncharted territory, and we are going to lose you soon."

I barely have time to enter the last of the codes when I feel the ship tilt to its side. I open the viewer in front of me and panic. Swirling right in front of me is a wormhole. If the ship gets sucked through that, who knows where I will end up, if I even survive once it spits us out.

I fight the Traveler, trying to wrestle the controls away from her, but she is overriding every sequence I put in. I can barely hear SoL giving her commands, but she still is not responding. I look up at the holo screen and can see the worried look on SoL's face.

"SoL, this wormhole came out of nowhere and we are being pulled in!"

. . .

THE WHOLE SHIP SHUDDERS AS THE CONTROLS ARE JERKED OUT OF my hands. Everything starts to twirl, and I shut my eyes as I grip onto the captain's chair beneath me. The pressure in the cabin becomes suffocating, and I panic as the air feels like it is crushing my lungs. The ship tilts further to its side, and a sudden jerk slams my head back. I scream because it feels like my whole body is being turned inside out. My very last thought is of Katherine.

CHAPTER 4

RAZ

The feeling of someone caressing my cheek awakens me. I jerk my eyes open only to see Katherine fading away, her arms reaching out for me. She smiles sadly right before she completely vanishes. I roar, lunging for her and hitting the floor hard where she was just standing. I have no idea what happened, but my heart feels like it has been ripped right out of my chest with her disappearance.

My mind struggles with what I just saw. She felt so real and it takes me a moment to clear my head. *What the frack just happened?* I slowly pick myself up off the floor and shake my wings out behind me. I must have fallen hard on my right one as my wing base feels sore.

I make my way to the main console only to find it dark.

"SoL, Tordan, are you there? Traveler, this is your captain speaking. Report coordinates and damage now."

Opening the front viewer manually, I find myself staring at a dark planet.

"Traveler, reboot and advise on coordinates!"

I slam my hand down on the console when I realize the ship has gone completely offline, or the AI has been damaged. I attack the manual controls. I need to see if the ship has been compromised any further, as we had a hull breach right before we were sucked into whatever that was. I have no idea where we are or whether I can even access the files to manually fly this thing now.

I feel something warm flowing down the side of my head and I reach up, only to see it is my own, bright red blood. Lord of Light, give me strength as I cannot afford to get damaged out here. Once I get into the system, I am relieved to see that all the gravity sensors and the life support are still working so I know the ship is still performing its basic protocols.

Now, if I can only figure out how to unlock these flight controls. I need to see where the frack that black hole spat me out. I no more than think this when I see a small, bright object floating right toward us. Since I cannot fly this thing right now it is going to impact us at any time.

I continue going through screen after screen until I find the last download from Falcor that Tordan was trying to send me right before everything went black. It seems like it is only partially downloaded, but I have the schematics and every good pilot knows how to adapt. I pull the main flight controls up and rip the bottom of the console out. All the connectors are neat and lined up perfectly; looks like we are going to have to do some remodeling.

Taking one of my claws, I start pulling the wires out of the main brain of the AI. A few tugs and plugs later, I hear the thruster fire up, and the control deck comes back online.

"See brothers, I am not just another pretty face," I say to absolutely no one. The manual flight controls emerge from the console, and I take control of the ship. The coordinates have not been updated yet though, so I am still flying blind.

A flash of silver outside the view screen catches my eye again and as the thing gets closer, I can tell it is a machine of some sort. It is simply spinning around and around and appears to be out of control. I do a quick scan of it, looking for anything organic, but the scans show nothing alive inside this odd machine. I maneuver the Traveler and use one of the robotic arms to reach out and grab the object, trying not to damage our outer panels.

I pull it into the cargo bay and set the ship to hover mode. I do not want us free-floating in an unknown or uncharted area, but this contraption was made by something or someone. Maybe it will have some useful information, because I will take anything I can get right now.

I walk toward the cargo hold, my whole body twitching like I have been in a sparring match with SoL and lost. I stop as I walk down Traveler's long hallway, checking on random flashing lights as I go. Now that the AI is no longer watching over the basic operations, the smallest thing could quickly become a disaster.

I make sure the main shuttle door is closed before I enter the cargo bay. The machine is larger than it looked from the viewer and I approach it hesitantly. It seemed like a good idea at the time to bring it onto the ship, but now I am not sure how to proceed.

I barely have time to jump out of the way when it falls onto its side. A panel falls off the exterior and a bright yellow disk emerges, spinning slowly. A faint sound starts, then picks up in volume.

"Greetings! I am a representative from the planet Earth. My name is Voyager, and if you are listening to this, then we have finally made contact."

What are the odds that I would find something from Earth out here in the middle of nowhere?

Without the help of the Traveler's AI, I need to rely on myself to pull the information out of the machine manually. There are multiple ports next to its main computer, but none are compatible with anything I have on hand.

The prerecorded information on the machine from Earth that was playing from the bright disk simply played on repeat it would not stop. Only after I cut its main power supply and rewired it to a separate control panel did I find the coordinates I have been hunting for.

But without a current star chart, I am still flying blind, as I have no reference point to navigate by. Once I pull all the information I can find out of the object, I reinsert the bright disk and re-launch it into space as I have no way of storing it. At least with the information it held, I know I am in the right galaxy now.

I return to the main control room, grasping my sides as hunger bears down on me. I am going to have to tap into my reserves and I know it. I was supposed to be asleep during this part of the journey, but until I figure out where I am, I cannot slumber.

The problems just keep piling up. How am I going to get us home if by some miracle I find them? After I scrubbed as much information as I could from that machine, I thought it could not hurt to send out random frequencies to see if I could at least pick up ANDI. Even if I can get a partial lock on them, I will feel better. Right now, I am pulling at invisible strings as I try to figure out which direction to head.

I am staring at nothing when the proximity alert goes off again. *What the frack is it this time?* I fire the thrusters up and move the ship around, trying to see what possible disaster is on the horizon now, only to come face to face with what looks like a mass of metal machines.

Apparently, the one I pulled in was just one of many. I immediately start forming a plan in my mind, and I feel a new surge of energy rush through me. This mission is not dead yet, and as long as I have a single breath left in me, I am not going to stop until I find a way to get to her.

I contemplate how I will get the information I need from these crafts, since I cannot fit all of them into the cargo bay. A few are flying at higher speeds than others and I let those pass by as I grab onto two of the smaller ones. It takes some maneuvering, but with the information I have from the first one, I manage to rig up a plug that seems standard on each of these.

I feel like I am in a simulator as I miss the connection time and again. I almost cheer for myself when I finally get the plug inserted into the smallest one first. I refuse to sit out here and do nothing. One of these must include a more detailed star chart or coordinates. As I pull the information off each one, I become more intrigued by their contents and the minds that have decided this is the information to be embedded in the machines.

Satellites are what they are called, and so far, all the ones I have managed to pull anything from are all explorers of some sort. Whether they were sent out to rotate around specific planets or to simply take pictures of their solar system, they are all unique.

I have been shown what they call television, something else called commercials, and all types of music. There are so many different cultures you could take your pick on where to live or what you want to believe in. Through the last few risings, or days, as the humans call them, I have laughed multiple times as my translator tries to figure out some of this human slang.

I set the last satellite free and try to program all this information into the server still running on the Traveler. The holo comm flashes on and I swear I hear my father's voice for a moment, *"STOP,"* is the word I hear.

My heart jerks in my chest as I slide the chair away from the console and stand up. How many times in my life have I heard him say, *"When you do not know what direction to go in, STOP. Do not keep making bad decisions; figure out what it is going to take for you to succeed before you take a single step forward."*

I step back and run my fingers through my long hair. I know the answers are right here in front of me. "Katherine, I could sure use some help here", I whisper to no one ... it is not like she can hear me.

CHAPTER 5

KATHERINE

Everything I have come to love or ever known is being destroyed around me and I'm completely helpless to stop it. I stand on top of this mountain range and look out over the devastation around me.

No one saw this coming, and if they did, the human race had no way of halting it. I will never forget the day the government interrupted every TV program and texted all cell phones with the announcement: a huge asteroid had hit Jupiter. At first, they thought the impact had only done minor damage to the huge planet. But then images from Juno, a satellite orbiting in that part of the solar system, started coming back.

The impact crater was so huge that it knocked Jupiter off its axis and its orientation within the solar system. Debris from the collision spewed out of Jupiter's atmosphere, wreaking havoc on Saturn, Mars, and bombarding both planets nonstop.

Within two days of the impact, we started seeing random asteroids in our skies, and then the unthinkable happened. Jupiter's extreme gravity started pulling all the planets towards it, and we ... I mean, Earth started moving.

It's been a little over a year now and it's like we've been reset from a modern, innovative and creative culture to a primitive and violent one. The first few months were plagued by impacts from the wreckage, fires, tsunamis, and massive flooding. From day to day, we didn't know if we were going to survive the bombs from the sky since they were almost impossible to detect until it was too late to have people evacuate the area. We lost over a third of the Earth's population in weeks, including my aunt and uncle who were in the Amazon jungle at the time. I felt it the moment they were killed; their spirits racing together across the heavens, laughing in their unique, mischievous way as they chased each other into the in-between.

After what seemed like forever, the United Nations finally unified every country and for the first time in Earth's history, everyone was working toward the same goal ... survival of our planet. Satellites were deployed and the missile station in space was activated. They managed to keep the skies clear for a few weeks and the people were hopeful that they had found a way to halt the destruction. Scientists said that the Earth would stop being pulled out of its own orbit because our gravity field was stronger than Jupiter's. They also said that we had already experienced the worst of it.

They were wrong.

I laugh to myself now because hours later, the storms started. Tornadoes touched down in places that had never seen them before ... Hurricanes were so intense that nothing survived in their paths ... Earthquakes rumbled underground, toppling whole cities in hours. The few survivors in those places that tried to unite and rebuild were killed by looters and criminals. There was no place that was safe anymore.

After quite a bit of discussion, Uncle Ty brought us all here to his mountain and to what was left of his ship, ANDI. So far, the ship has withstood the things that have been thrown at it and even managed to anchor farther into the mountain when we started experiencing earthquakes here too.

Even though we all had to walk away from our current way of life, we've managed to adjust. I guess after being alive for so many years, like Uncle Ty, you don't become as attached because you've seen nothing but change as the years go by.

But my whole foundation is shifting under me as I watch my mother and my best friend fade right in front of me. We've always been tied to the very essence the earth provides us with. Mother Earth's fiery personality feeds our own, but Mom has always been directly linked to her.

I didn't notice it at first, or maybe I didn't want to. We had just lost Rage and we were all devastated. I had felt his exhaustion, but I was able to collect his spirit as his physical body died, and I was going to hold onto his soul until I could reincarnate him. He had lived for over a thousand years, and he was so weary. Letting him go was one of the hardest decisions I've ever had to make, and if I'd known my mother's lifespan had been tied directly to his, I would've never let him pass.

I think back to the very first time I saw a gray hair on her head and how I teased her horribly about it. I didn't realize she was starting to age. Mom always had an inner spark, a playfulness that offset my dad's seriousness. I spent my entire childhood and then my whole adult life surrounded by their love for one another.

I came to this mountain today searching for a moment of clarity as I've watched Mom age years in the last few weeks. Small laugh lines appeared on her face, and I had to hold back tears the other day when she stumbled on a set of stairs and sprained her ankle ... a first for her.

I don't know what to do. She was my best friend first and then she became my mother. How do I let her spirit go when I have no way of holding her in this world? Will I be able to find her in the great beyond if I set her free? And then there's dad. He won't make it an hour without her; I'll lose them both.

I hear her moments before I feel her standing behind me. I feel comforted instantly the moment she takes my hand.

"I figured I would find you here. Even with all the destruction, there are still pieces like this that remind us of the true beauty she has always provided for us. What has you so troubled, Kat?"

"Where do I start? To be honest, Mom? Thoughts of you and dad ... what's gonna happen next ... who is RaZ? I know in my heart he's mine, but that doesn't make us compatible. We're complete strangers with a similar goal. What will change if he does make it here? What's going to happen to everything I've ever known? Do I really want to leave? Can we find a way to stay? Would he stay here with me if that's what I chose to do? So many questions that I don't have the answers to and no way of knowing. I'm surrounded by people I love, but my heart knows everything is going to change and I'm terrified!"

"Come, walk with me."

Mom doesn't say anything as we walk along the top of the ridge. Ghost and Glory play up ahead of us as we walk hand in hand. Mom stops for a second reaching up to pull a wilted leaf off a tree.

"Can you feel it?"

"What Mom?"

"She's dying?"

"The tree?"

"No, the Earth. Her death has slowed down momentarily, but I have a feeling things are getting ready to quickly shift for the worse. Her core is gradually slowing down because of our displacement from the sun. That's why we lost Rage and the others so quickly. She called them back to her and it won't be long before she does the same to me."

"Mom! I can..."

"NO! Now, let me finish because I know you can see the changes in me. Your father is in complete denial, but you need to come to the realization that we will not be going with you on the next adventure in your life."

"What are you talking about? I'm not leaving here without you! That was never an option."

Mom runs her hand down my cheek and smiles sadly at me. "Baby, she isn't going to let me leave. She's already pulling her life essence from all of her children. You must promise me that the day I leave this world, you will let me go. I was blessed with you and your dad. I've had a thousand years of laughter and love that only a handful of others can understand. Now it's your turn to live."

"You expect me to simply stand back and lose both of my parents at the same time when I have a way to save you? Because you know dad won't make it an hour without you."

"I'm asking as your mother and your best friend for you to let us go. As it is, you're going to have a hard enough time escaping the clutches the earth has on you. There's no way you'll be able to hold onto our souls for such an extended period of time. I know you ... If you lost us afterward, you would never forgive yourself. You need to concentrate on yourself.

Lord Kat, you're a mix of both of us. If you make it, you'll take the best of us with you. Your ability to walk between the living and the dead to help us stay or pass on is amazing, and it doesn't even include the longevity of the vampire genes you got from your father. Or the fiery temper you got from me and my Hellhound essence. I only pray the other two traits in you are stronger than the abilities you got from me. Because you may have a fight on your hands once you're in space and no longer attached to the Earth as we are now. Your dad and his marvelous mind are the ones who spotted this problem. Dad and Ty have been trying to work through it ever since.

You have no idea what a burden was lifted from me the moment I saw your RaZ in that communication. The way he looked at you, if he could have leaped through the screen to get to you, he would have. I know in my heart that young man is doing everything in his power to make it here to you. It does my heart good to know that you'll have him.

Katherine, you have to make me a promise. If he comes, and you know he will, you will leave here and not look back. Yes, you are of this world, but you are also so much more. Your ties to the earth will make it difficult to leave, and I'm not sure how to prepare you for the trials you'll face, but you will prevail. I can see it ... you in another place, but it's not fully clear in my mind."

"Mom, we don't even know if he'll make it and if he does, there are just too many IFs."

"I have been watching you the last few days. You can feel him, can't you?"

"My mind seeks him out. There are times I feel like I'm practically standing right in front of him, and then others ... I don't know how to explain it. I've seen things, things in my life, like I'm looking through his eyes and not mine. I've felt him moving closer every day, but it's like he's lost.

I woke up the other night and I could've sworn for just a second that I was standing next to him. I reached out and touched his cheek, and he jerked straight up looking right at me. I could feel the heat coming off his skin. Then he was gone, but I know he's coming. Let's just pray it's not too late."

"Have you mentioned this to Ty? It may be time to try to send a signal out. I want you off this rock as soon as possible."

Mom has no more than said that when the ground under our feet starts to tremble. Off in the distance, I can see trees crumbling to the ground as the massive mountain in front of us seems to implode in on itself. I grab her arm and flash us to the bottom of the hill, only a few feet from the front door of Ty and Vic's house.

Father appears at the door before I can open it, pulling us inside. Remembering Glory and Ghost were playing on the hill in front of me, I start to turn back to get them when something hits me from behind and I crumple to the floor.

CHAPTER 6

RAZ

For months now, I have captured as many of these satellites as I can. Without the Traveler's AI, I have had to splice the information together myself. After a few mistakes, I believe I am finally on the right track, and at my current speed, I should see Earth's galaxy soon.

There has not been a single indication that I was even on the right path until I finally got some real data from that last machine. The star charts have been so incomplete to this point that I am simply heading toward their sun, hoping to recognize some of the planets on the way. I look out the viewer as I'm getting ready to pass the largest planet I have encountered so far. Its gravitational pull is so weak that it does not even have any visible impact craters on its surface. If these star charts are correct, I should be coming upon a massive debris field shortly. The planets they call Saturn and Jupiter should be the next ones in line, but I have no idea if they are still anywhere near their last coordinates.

If my calculations are right, I am still a lunar rotation away from Earth at my current speed. Because of the limited control functions I have been able to access, I have no idea if I have enough power left in the main energy banks to use the thrusters at full max. I am already closer than we thought I would be at this time, but I was supposed to be asleep right now. I can feel my body becoming sluggish from the lack of nourishment. It has taken all my willpower not to go into the galley and feast upon the last of the remaining blood packets.

I am walking over to the final satellite I was able to capture when I suddenly feel something. A heavy weight settles upon my shoulders, pushing me to my knees. It takes me a moment to realize there is nothing on me. I shake my head trying to clear the sudden fuzziness surrounding me. *What the frack just happened?*

I stand up, shaking my wings out in agitation. I have been experiencing things like this for days now. Being alone here, I have become melancholy. The days, or in my world rotations, are all blending together; time has become my nemesis as the next rising seems so far away.

I throw the tools in my hand down and head to my private chamber. The door slides open, and I hit the proximity alarm next to the sleeping platform and then simply fall face-first into its softness. My mind is tired, but my body is restless and hunger gnaws at my insides like a parasite trying to eat me from the inside out.

I no sooner closed my eyes when I find myself hovering above another sleeping platform, a bed I believe it is called. The place is unfamiliar to me, but not the figure laying there. Long, straight black hair hangs down past her shoulders, her features softened by sleep as she lays there peacefully. A light blanket covers her completely, so her slim body is hidden from me. I catch a glimpse of others in the room, but I cannot make out who they are.

I sense fear and worry surrounding the female ... my Katherine. I call out her name, but she does not move. She seems unharmed, but also nonresponsive. A large gray animal lays protectively at her side. He must sense me and looks up and snarls, his eyes flashing red as he must see me as a threat. I watch another female approach the bed. She runs a hand down the aggressive animal's back.

"Be good Ghost, or I'll make you go back outside!"

I hover back out of the way when I see a male approach the bed from the other side. I hold back the growl that wants to leave my throat when he touches her forehead lightly.

"Emma, she is burning up, and she has never been sick a day in her life!"

"Lucas, I don't know what to do! I haven't left her side since that compression wave from the mountain imploding knocked her down. She saved my life up there. I was so absorbed by what was happening in front of me that I didn't think about the danger we were in.

When she first started feeling warm, I had ANDI prepare a cool bath for her. I thought it was working, but then the water began to steam from her body's heat. I'm truly scared she'll never wake, and it's not like we can call a doctor. Ty's even clueless as to why she isn't coming around. All his scans show she's healthy, except for this high fever. To be honest, I fear the destruction all around us is finally affecting her. I have felt her OTHERS in the room here with us. What if they take her? She has so much to live for, and I'm scared that my telling her that we weren't going to leave with her may affect her judgment."

The male finally turns my way and the first glimpse of his face shocks me. Even though he seems paler than most of the humans I have witnessed up to this point, you can see his features are not of this world. He pulls the other woman close, hugging her tightly. She says something to him that I cannot hear, and he smiles down at her, his fangs showing clearly.

I am so shocked, I do not know how to react. He is just like me, minus the wings. Am I not the only one of my kind? How has this happened? I have so many questions.

Something touching my wing has me twisting away from the scene in front of me. Katherine runs her hand gently down the appendage, caressing it lovingly.

"These are beautiful. I can't imagine the sights you've been able to see and experience because of the abilities these give you."

I try to talk, but nothing comes out. It is like my words are stuck in my head no matter how hard I try to respond.

She points to the couple in the room with her.

"Those are my parents. I have watched them my whole life and their love for one another has never dimmed. Until recently, they have always acted like two teenagers. I'm watching them fade right before my eyes. I'm being forced to choose ... you or them. No child should be made to do that!"

She lets go of my wing with a sad smile on her face, floating away from me and back toward her body lying on the bed. I reach for her as the urge to hold her in my arms is almost overwhelming, but my arms pass right through her. I try once again only for the same thing to happen as she seems to be fading right before me. Katherine does not seem to notice as she watches her parents intently. I can barely hear her as her next words seem to float to me from a long distance.

"RaZ, you must hurry. The Earth is cooling and when it reaches a certain point, everything we know will be destroyed from within. My own body is reacting to the fires beneath us. The spirits are trying to warn me of the pain I'm going to experience. They want me to join them in the beyond, and in the last few days, it has been tempting to let go. My whole family will be there soon. I would be with them for eternity, forever to be held in their embrace. The only thing that's holding me here right now is ... you."

The scene in front of me starts to fade as I feel my body being pulled away.

I jerk awake. It takes me a minute to remember where I am as the sight I just witnessed plays back in my mind. There must be a quicker way for me to get to her. I jump up, a sudden plan forming in my head.

I grab the holo screen Tordan sent me and start going through the schematics. I need information on the main thrusters to ensure I have enough power to fire them at full capacity. I walk through the ship, darkening rooms and turning off unnecessary operations. I dump the satellites in the holding bay back into space and double-check my charted course.

One of the last things I do is grab a bag of blood out of the warmer, practically inhaling the small bag. My mind and body instantly feel more alert: I needed that boost to get me through the next few rotations.

Sitting down at the controls, I slowly start powering up two of the thrusters. I leave the third one off in case of an emergency, or if I feel like I need a boost to get away from something.

I look down to see which gauges I have managed to get working and everything seems to be in the green. I push the throttle forward and the ship accelerates quickly. As we clear our first planet, I can plainly see the destruction in front of me. That asteroid destroyed practically this entire solar system with one fatal strike.

After seeing the destruction, there is no way I will be leaving the controls anytime soon. I will have to find a way through all this debris. The only thing working in my favor is that it seems like the largest planet is heading away from me and its gravity is so strong it's pulling a lot of the damage along with it.

I set the deflector shields to max capacity and start my way through this maze of rock and ash. The ship is handling beautifully, responding with just a flick of my wrist when we approach obstacles in our flight path. I send out a beacon, hoping that Grandfather's AI picks it up soon because I need the coordinates to their location, or I will be flying around their planet for days. I know we do not have that kind of time to waste.

CHAPTER 7

KATHERINE

The warmth settled on my side comforts me as I fight my way out of the in-between I have been in for days now. I feel Ghost bump my side as he realizes I'm awake. Lifting my hand up, I run it down his thick fur. His low growl has me opening my eyes. One of the other hounds has entered the room and is approaching the bed. He's always so territorial, even with Glory, and they have been together for hundreds of years now. But he's even worse if it's one of the males. Thorn acts like he's going to jump on the end of the bed, and I can't hold back the giggle that leaves my throat when Ghost knocks him back to the floor. I see Thorn start to puff up.

"Ok, you two knock it off."

I can smell Dad's cologne before he enters the room.

"It's about time you returned, young lady. You gave us quite a scare there. I'm not used to my little girl being down, let alone unconscious."

He motions for Ghost to get off the bed, and once he hops down, Dad sits in his place. He reaches up and pushes a piece of my hair off my forehead.

"Do you remember what happened?"

"Mom and I were up on the mountaintop. We were talking, and then out of nowhere, I sensed danger all around us. I remember grabbing Mom and flashing us home, but that's it."

I look away from his all-knowing eyes and glance out the window. The sky was an eerie yellow color, and it is screaming danger.

"It looks like we have a bad storm coming."

"You have always done that."

"What?"

"Changed the subject if you didn't want to talk about something. I understand that you were upset after talking to your mother, but you must realize we didn't make this decision lightly. There is nothing either of us would rather do than follow you to the ends of the world. If we thought there was any way to do it, we would. You have to know how much we love you, Kat."

"I do, Dad. I just feel like the two of you have given up. So, what... you've started to age. People get old all the time, but they make the best of it. You guys are forcing me to make a choice that I don't know I'm capable of. I mean, do I stay in this world I know, surrounded by people who love me, even if it's for a short time? Or do I leave for the unknown with a man I have only seen in my dreams? Dad, I know absolutely nothing about him. And I'm supposed to allow him to take me away from everything that's dear to me? Now, don't get me wrong, I'm extremely happy Uncle Ty finally gets to go home. He deserves that after all these years, and we all know he'll go out of his way to make sure Aunt Vic adjusts well.

But RaZ will be expecting me to go with him, especially after all he's gone through to get here. And that may be ok after I get to know him better, but right now it's not. I'm scared, Dad. I thought I would at least have you and Mom ... and if we were all together, I could work through anything, but I'm not that strong on my own. I won't have anyone to lean on or go to if this fails. And who will I vent to when he drives me crazy?"

Dad gets up and starts pacing the room.

"I'm calling bullshit, Kat. You're just looking for excuses. You're an amazing young woman with a heart of gold. Any man would be lucky to call you theirs. To be honest, I was beginning to worry that you'd never find that special someone to share your long life with. Mom and I have watched you date, but we knew the moment you left the house, your heart wasn't in it. You should be looking at this as a new adventure, honey, not some menial task to get through. If what they are saying is true, you will have years before you set foot on his planet. You'll know way before you ever get there where your heart lies. And if it's not with this RaZ, you will have multitudes to pick from if Tyberius' stories prove true.

I think back to the day I picked your mother up off the ground all those years ago. If you had told me right then that the pitiful creature in my arms was my destiny and that I would come to love her to the point of obsession, I would have given you a good cussing and run like hell. None of us adapts well to change, baby."

Red tears flow down my cheeks, and I brush them away, hoping dad doesn't see how upset I am as I try to hold the rest of them back.

He comes back to the bed and pulls me into his chest, hugging me tightly. His familiar arms and the comfort they have always given me break what strength I had left, and I can no longer hold the sobs back. He cradles my head as he rocks me back and forth. Dad doesn't say a word; he simply lets me cry. After what feels like forever, I finally calm down. He pulls back from me, gently wiping the few tears I have left off my face and kisses me on the forehead.

"You know that your mother and I will truly never leave you, honey. We'll always watch over you no matter the distance. When the time comes, and throughout your life, it will, you need to remember how we've all been blessed and draw strength from that. We've had centuries full of love and laughter that most can only dream of. If you feel like your life here will fade over time, maybe while you're on this long trip through the stars, you should write down our family's story. This will give you something to share with your young ones one day. And that way ... our story will live on forever."

He kisses my forehead once again and then lowers me back down, covering me up.

"Clear your mind little one and be at ease. There is nowhere you need to be today. I love you!"

Dad walks out of the room and Ghost jumps back up on the bed. He pushes his head up under my arm and then lays it on my shoulder. His cold, wet nose bumps my chin; this is his normal way to tell me he loves me too. I gather him close and stare out the window, contemplating Dad's words with a heavy heart. Change sucks!

CHAPTER 8
TYBERIUS AND VICTORIA

I have been watching the storms outside intensify over the last few hours. We have never experienced any kind of tornadoes or massive flooding here in the mountains, but these storms look different.

Victoria walks into the room and I'm so deep in thought about the upcoming trip and the possible problems we may encounter on the way that I don't acknowledge her right away. The excitement and possibility that I may be able to go home after centuries on this planet has made me overlook the blessings it has provided for me through all these long years. I have been distant, especially to the one standing right in front of me.

I see Vic start to turn away, a rare frown upon her face. I reach out and grab her arm before she can take another step away from me and pull her in close. She wraps her arms around my waist tightly and lets out a sigh. I kiss the top of her head as I realize that maybe she wasn't the only one who needed a hug.

"What's the matter, Angel?"

"Nothing Ty. You have enough on your plate right now, so you don't need to worry about me too."

She pulls away and looks up at me sadly. "But what isn't there to worry about? I don't know where to start and I'm sure the things that are bothering me are petty compared to the things coursing through that big brain of yours."

"Let's talk about them, love, and see if we can't eliminate some of them. Your concerns are important to me. I've let you down as a mate if you feel that your concerns are not as important or valid as mine."

"Oh, quit it ... you've never let me down! I love you more than I can express, and you know it. I'm just so worried about the unknown and if I'm being honest, I'm not sure being stuck in a small box for years is something I can manage. I'm terrified by the mere thought of being surrounded by the darkness I know we'll face in space. I'm truly frightened and I haven't even seen it. I can already feel its cold seeping into my bones, and we're not even on the ship yet. I'm also worried about how we're going to feed everyone; can we even store enough blood for that long?

Then, if by the grace of God we do manage to get to your home, you'll become a celebrity, the ancient one who made it. You'll be the famous survivor who managed to live for centuries on a primitive planet. Your peers will all want to know your story and about your experiences. You're going to be so busy that there'll be no time for me. Now, I don't begrudge you your moment in the spotlight because you deserve it. But where does that leave me? You know how uncomfortable I am in crowds. It's not going to be like here where I can always flash home if I'm overwhelmed.

And another problem ... I'm sure you were declared dead, so you'll have to go through all that headache. And in the meantime, where will we live? Here on Earth, you're a billionaire because of your trades and experience. Not to mention that you've had a few years to obtain your fortune, but I don't believe human money is transferable. So, we're going to be broke unless there's something you haven't told me? If the discussion we had about your old life and planet was honest, you worked in a library.

I know you've spoiled me all these years and it's not that I'm not willing to work, but what am I going to do in an alien world? How will Kat and I ever fit into your world? I can see the stress all over her as well as you. Ty, we're all at a breaking point here. I hate the unknown and I hate change, but this is a little bigger than moving to another state or changing the wallpaper, don't you think? It's not like if we're unhappy, we can just come back to Earth for a quick visit or vacation."

I can't help it, but I start laughing. She's terrified and she hasn't said a word until now. As she would say, *bless her heart*!

"Is that all honey? I may need a big notebook to write all of this down."

Victoria hits me playfully on the arm.

"Stop making fun of me, I'm serious."

"I know you are and I'm not laughing at you, I'm laughing with you, angel. I don't know all the answers, but I promise we won't starve. I have enough money to keep us comfortable no matter what planet we're on. I'm sure there will be time, once we're closer to Darverius, to work out all the paperwork, as you put it. One thing you will have to get used to is that there will be no flashing from one point to another on Darverius. The gravity is denser there and that was an ability I didn't even know was possible until I did it by mistake here on Earth.

As for you and Katherine, there are other human females on Darverius. I can't wait to hear the stories of how they came to be there because technically, they shouldn't be. And there are so many species on the planet, you will simply be one more oddity to some and a rarity to others. We will know more when I can finally communicate with DaR.

I promise, it will not be all doom and gloom. My home plant is beautiful, and we will get to explore and do things that I was never able to do with you here on Earth. I know leaving everything that you've ever known is going to be hard. To be completely honest with you, I've come to love this place too. After all, it gave me you and Kat and so many others through the years to love and care for."

Victoria runs her hand down my cheek.

"I noticed that you just said Kat and me. So, you've heard Lucas and Emma talking about not going with us?"

"They came to me a few nights ago, asking for my opinion. But in the long run, it is their lives and their decision."

"Will we start aging once we get to Darverius?"

"Not right away, no, but I don't believe we will have the immortality we have been blessed with here on Earth. I will also have to find a substitute blood supply for us once we get there as we don't have the same type of animals there as we do here."

I hear Victoria sigh as she turns away from me.

"Ty, you know you honestly haven't given me a single reason to want to go there."

"If the Earth weren't moments from destroying itself, I would have never asked it of you. We can stay if you wish. I will never leave you, ever ... no matter what. And if you decide that you want to stay, to take our chances here, then we will. We'll make the best of it and enjoy what time we have left."

"I'm sorry Ty, and you're right, it doesn't matter where we are as long as we're together. We will go on this next adventure together and I'll be fine because I have you by my side. Now my last question ... if there's room, have you thought about taking anyone else, especially since Lucas and Emma aren't going?"

"I haven't really thought past our immediate family. I released everyone from all our estates when the destruction started. We will see when the time comes, as this may be something we should all talk about together."

The sound of a loud alarm echoes throughout the room and I turn to the screen, quickly turning it off. I plug ANDI back in and pray he has enough life left in him to lead RaZ to us, because that was his ship sending out a ping to contact us.

I motion for Victoria once I turn off the alarm.

"Go tell the others the good news, as I believe we can all use some right now. And let's see if ANDI has a little magic left in his old soul because I believe that's RaZ trying to locate us."

CHAPTER 9

RAZ

Out of nowhere and just when I was getting ready to turn the beacon off, I get a ping. It's so faint that I almost didn't catch it, but every minute it gets louder. I have tried to send out an audio, but I can tell they cannot hear me as there seems to be tons of interference.

The debris field has become so thick that I can only leave the cockpit for a few moments at a time. I am down to three bags of blood, and my body seems to be reacting more slowly than usual. Pushing the Traveler to her max these past few days should at least put Earth in my sight soon. Suddenly, something is pushing me hard. Not only do I need food, but I also feel time is of the essence.

I come around the side of a red planet that seems to be cracking in half and there in front of me is what I have been hunting for, Earth. At first, I was worried I would not know what to look for and that I would simply fly past their planet. But it is very clear that this planet once supported a thriving environment. I can see large ash clouds and massive storms lighting up its atmosphere. Red cracks seem to be forming, cutting the planet in half. One side still seems to support life, but anything on the other side would have been destroyed.

I will not reach her planet for another few rotations at this speed, but being able to see it is a wonderful feeling. I cannot believe I have made it this far. Years of searching for something I was not sure I could find has made my journey feel unreal.

There is enough cleared space in front of the ship that I can take a quick ionizing shower. I would hate for Katherine's first impression of me to be, '*He stinks!*' I re-enter the cockpit and decide to fire up the final thruster ... frack it with waiting more rotations. The ship lurches forward and I watch as the planet gets closer. I once again send out an audio message, trying to let them know I am coming, but I receive nothing but static in return. Within hours, I am directly above the last coordinates I received from ANDI and there is a massive storm headed this way if my calculations are correct.

The number of satellites freely floating around the planet is astounding. All of this technology ... simply wasted.

I turn off two of the three thrusters to slow down the massive ship until I can get her into an actual orbit. Here she will hover until I return. SoL made sure the Traveler was equipped with two personal shuttles that I can fly back and forth as the Traveler is too large to be docked on land. Once I have her locked in place, I head toward the shuttle bay. My wings twitch behind me as my body is flooded with adrenaline.

I remotely fire up one of the shuttles from the cockpit of the main ship. She sits with her main door open, floating inches above the floor waiting for me. I walk up the short ramp and head straight to the captain's chair. After I lock onto the signal, I open the shuttle bay and I cannot stop the shout that leaves my throat when we shoot out into open space.

We break through Earth's atmosphere, effortlessly flying above the clouds. I make sure to keep my ship cloaked until I can find a safe place to land as I have no idea how the humans will react. I am also worried about how I am going to hide my wings; it is not like I can cover them up with something. I fly directly over the coordinates, not recognizing anything. I was hoping for a large dwelling or something that would indicate I was near civilization, but there is nothing here but mountains.

I find a clearing large enough to set the ship down. I then program it to relaunch to a safe altitude, way above the clouds and incoming storms. The last thing I need is for my shuttle to be damaged and for all of us to be stuck with no way to reach the Traveler. If the AI was still functioning, I would be in constant contact with the ship, but unfortunately, that is not the case. I hope that between my grandfather and me, we will have enough combined knowledge to get us back home.

I open the doorway and launch into the sky, practically gagging as the air itself smells like destruction. The very essence of the planet seems wrong to me ... like it is a ticking bomb on its final countdown. But it feels wonderful to be back in the air again. Unfortunately, because of the difference in gravity, I must watch my surroundings as I seem to be flying over the ground faster than usual.

I hear a crack of lightning behind me, and as I turn, something on the ground catches my attention. There is a group of small Selin, no wait, a minute, I know what the humans call these ... They are wolves, canines...running through the trees below me. I catch a glimpse of someone running with them, but the moment I hear the female's laughter, my heart practically stops. I know immediately who that is.

I see a group of trees buckling ahead of them and I tuck my wings in and dive in her direction. She is steps away from a tree falling on her when I snatch her up in my arms and fly straight back into the sky, out of harm's way.

Everything happens so quickly she does not have time to react. I flap my wings, hovering a few feet above the tree line and then I look down. The sight of her bright green eyes and the smile on her face makes my heart jerk inside my chest.

"Hello beautiful, where have you been my whole life?"

"Apparently, waiting for you to get your ass here. What took you so long?"

"Delayed flight."

She throws her head back and laughs and I pull that sound ... her very soul, into my own. She pulls one of her arms out from between us, where I have pulled her in close to me, and curls her hand around the back of my neck. Before I realize what she is doing, she pulls my head down, capturing my lips with her own. The moment her lips touch mine. I almost forget we are flying and I actually drop us a few feet before my wings automatically catch us.

She pulls back looking up at me with a huge smile on her face. She starts to say something, but before she can get a word out, I pull her back to me. She giggles as I nibble and suck on her bottom lip. I feel like I am a slobbering youngling as I crush her body to mine. I kiss her with all the pent-up passion that I have been carrying inside me for years while I was searching for her. Nothing could have prepared me for the ecstasy of simply holding her in my arms.

When she wraps her legs around my waist, I put one hand under her delicious, round bottom and grip the back of her head, tilting it just right as I learn this human kiss. It is something I have looked forward to doing ever since I saw it on a satellite feed.

She moans in my arms when I start to kiss the side of her neck, but the pulse under her skin brings my hunger back full force and I make myself pull away. Katherine gazes up at me with desire in her eyes and if I could simply stay in this exact moment for eternity, I would. All the years of loneliness were worth it for this single moment in time.

"In all the ways I imagined first meeting you, I couldn't have ever dreamed this up," she whispers to me.

The storm seems to have passed as I have unknowingly flown us quite a distance away from where I picked her up. I see her look down as I slowly lower us to the ground. I wrap a wing around her, keeping her close and safe from the intense winds.

She puts her hand on my chest glancing up at me. "Wow, I could get used to that kind of transportation."

"I look forward to holding you in my arms indefinitely, but in my current weakened state, it is not safe. Are your lodgings close by? I will not leave you out here since everything around us appears unstable. I do not want to leave you at all, but I must find sustenance soon. My body is starving, and you are way too tempting. Your smell calls to me like no other, and I do not trust myself right now."

"Thank God you didn't try to. My blood is toxic, RaZ. No one has ever been able to feed from me and not get deathly sick."

"I think you are the sweetest smelling poison ever then." I laugh when she rolls her eyes at me.

She whistles loudly and I hear multiple feet pounding the ground as they come nearer to us.

"Don't worry, sweet talker, it's just my babies. When you first grabbed me, I had to let them know I was safe. Otherwise, they wouldn't have stopped until they found a way to get me away from you."

"Babies, as in plural?"

"Yeah, you'll see them shortly; I have three that seldom ever leave my side. They will seem a little much at first, but they really are just big babies that want to be loved on."

Three huge, canine-like animals come rushing at us and I grab Katherine, pushing her behind me. These look different from the ones I saw her with earlier. The animals stalk forward and they seem to be getting larger the closer they get. Huge fangs drip saliva on the ground as their large eyes pulse red. I hear a distinct growl from the male in the front.

This shocks me, as I am used to the females being the largest and the most terrifying on Darverius. I feel Katherine poke me in the shoulder.

"If you don't step aside, he will probably try to use these wings I'm currently fascinated with as chew toys. Ghost is extremely territorial!"

Before I can say a single word, she has stepped between me and the canines in front of me. The moment she is in front of me, the growling stops and the big animal pounces playfully around her. For a moment back there, he looked bigger to me than he does now.

She reaches back for my hand and pulls me forward. "RaZ let me introduce you to these three mongrels. The big guy up front is Ghost and we have been together since I was a small child. His female is Glory, and this handsome male is Thorn. He's their cousin. We've been looking for a female for him, but most of them perished some time back. We are all linked together emotionally and I can communicate with them through a form of telepathy unique to just us. That's how I was able to tell them that I was ok when you grabbed me."

"They are as impressive as my Selin, even though I am not sure how my Queens would react to such strong males." My stomach cramps and I fall to one knee. I force myself back to my feet, but not before I feel Katherine's warmth under one shoulder, as she forces me up. Her strength surprises me.

"Enough messing around, you need blood now."

"How did you know that is what I needed?"

"Honey, we all have the same diet!"

This time when she smiles at me, I see her small fangs emerge.

"How did you do that? Hide them, I mean."

"You will learn, I'm full of all kinds of surprises."

She whistles loudly and I pull away, startled. I watch all three canines spread out in front of us, the big male leading the way. He walks carelessly, but I can tell he is guarding us as we move forward.

We approach a huge door that looks as if it were carved right out of the side of the mountain. The door jerks open and standing in the doorway is an older, softer version of my father. I feel tears in my eyes as the man before me suddenly becomes real ... He has always been a name without a face. A being so beloved by my father that we all envied him somewhat. My grandfather.

I cannot seem to make a single sound and he is down the steps and standing in front of me before I can react. He grabs me up in a huge hug, picking me up off the ground and swinging me around like a youngling. Once he sets me back on my feet, I am a little overwhelmed as all of this happens in mere tics. He simply stands before me, studying me, looking me up and down. He reaches up as I am slightly taller and caresses my cheek.

"You favor your father so much it hurts to look upon your face ... I feel like I'm staring at a dream. All that I have missed is standing before me, and we have so much to discuss. I have prayed to the Lord of the Light for centuries. I thought he had turned his back on me, but he was simply saving all those prayers for this very moment in time."

I watch, mesmerized as a lone tear flows down his cheek.

For the first time in my life, I am speechless. What do you say to a legend? To the male who was responsible for making your own father into the very best being, who then, in turn, made all of us the males we are today. I can see the love on his face as he looks at me, a perfect stranger, but to him, I represent all that he left behind.

He waves me forward, "Come, I can feel your hunger. Let's get you fed, and then we will talk."

Standing a few steps above me, Katherine is just inside the doorway with her arm around another female. She is stunning in appearance, until she starts to turn away and there is no missing the scars marring one side of her beautiful face.

Before I think twice about what I am saying, I turn to grandfather. I nod my head toward the other female.

"I hope you destroyed whoever or whatever did that to her?"

"I didn't get the pleasure, as Katherine's mother had that honor. I'm shocked she let you see them. Normally, Victoria glamours herself if others are around. She is the reason I never gave up; she has become my everything. As I said, we have so much to discuss, but I fear we won't have long to do it here. The Earth is angry, and she is about to set forth on a course none will survive."

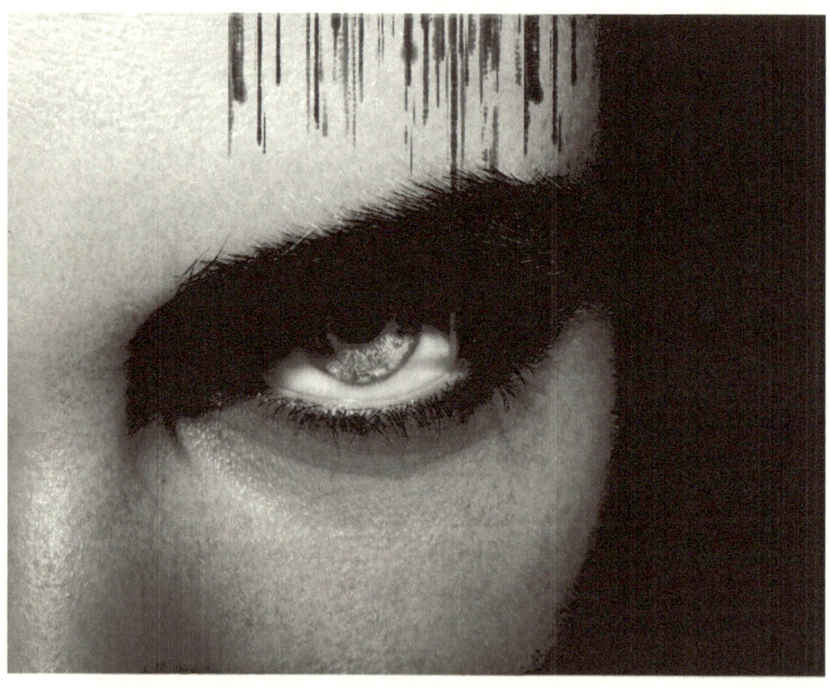

CHAPTER 10

RAZ

Katherine takes my hand leading me forward. I am so weak it is taking all my strength to take my next step. We come to a doorway, and the smell hits me before Grandfather even gets the door open.

He walks in first, then motions for me to come forward.

"I'm not sure about your current diet, but I'm assuming by those massive fangs of yours that the Blood Beet hasn't been enough to sustain you. This will taste a little different, but I promise your body will absorb it and you will feel better after a few bags."

I barely stop myself from simply snatching the bag out of his hands. Tearing the top open, I guzzle the warm blood down, emptying it in seconds. He holds another one out for me and it takes five bags before I feel like myself again.

I stretch my wings out as much as possible in this small room and my whole body seems to expand and fill out. Katherine does not say anything and they all simply stand to the side watching me. None of them seemed shocked by my body's reaction to the blood. I take a moment to catch my breath as it is nice to finally feel like myself again.

"Thank you! I knew I was cutting it close, but things happened that I could not control, and my supply ran out more quickly than I anticipated. My body was only rotations from shutting down. I would have been floating in space indefinitely if that had happened before I found you."

"RaZ, how long have you been consuming blood? I was expecting a different reaction from you when I handed you that bag."

"As you humans put it ... to make a long story short, I bit my mother shortly after my birth, and she panicked. They immediately contacted Father to come get his abomination, as they blamed his genes for what they thought was wrong with me. Father, of course, came for me immediately. He said I was inconsolable, that nothing they fed me would stay down.

Father said that during one darkness, he was pacing the floor with me, and that I bit his shoulder hard, my small fangs sinking so deep that I drew blood. He said I calmed down once I started consuming his blood. He pulled me away once he felt me sucking on his blood, thinking it would make me sick. Father said I cried so loudly that people on other planets could hear me. He immediately put me back on his shoulder, trying anything to console me, as no one real-ized at the time that I was starving.

He still has small fang marks on his right shoulder because I was too young to know how to heal them. He could not hand me over to anyone else because I was constantly looking for sustenance. It took me biting XuL once to make him realize I was going to need blood to survive or no one was going to be safe around my fangs. To say the least, I never went hungry again. I can eat some solid foods but not much."

"I notice that you are speaking English. How did you learn this? I saw a human female standing behind your father. Did she teach you?"

"No, I only met her a few times. I do have a translator that helped me pick up your English and quite a few other languages on what you call space junk. Your satellites are full of knowledge and entertainment; one of them even carries a golden record. It took some of your 'tinkering', but once I was able to make a compatible connector, the information was endless. Books, music, multiple languages. I have been completely fascinated by the fact that there are so many different variations of the same thing. It is like Earth's gods got bored with only one type of life form and decided to see how many they could make. So many shapes, colors, and personalities for such a primitive race.

I got to enjoy what humans call TV, and hearing so much music was enlightening. I was happy to have access to the information because it helped pass the time. I do not understand some of the English slang, but I have picked up quite a bit about the history and advancement of this amazing planet. It did take me several rotations to become comfortable with your language, and even though I know Father and Tordan will be able to understand you when we return, for safety reasons, I still recommend that everyone have a translator implanted, even if they learn our main language.

The different species presently living on Darverius are diverse. And as of right now, unfortunately, human females are highly sought after, especially after father destroyed the slave market. For that reason, they need to be protected at all times. Father never leaves Kira alone without a guard just for this reason."

Grandfather pats me on the shoulder.

"You will quickly learn that our females are no damsels in distress. Though they are smart enough to understand that they will no longer be in an environment where they are the most dangerous thing there. We have much to talk about."

"Yes, we do, and I know time is not on our side as I saw firsthand from space the amount of damage Jupiter is causing to your entire solar system."

"You just arrived and we still have a few things to work out before we can leave. You need some downtime, and I can see that Katherine's patience is wearing thin as she keeps pacing back and forth in front of the doorway. I will leave you two alone for a few hours."

I turn, only to find Katherine standing right behind me. Before she can react, I bend down and pick her up, hugging her tightly. "I cannot believe you are real!" I sink my nose into her hair and inhale the unique smell that is all Katherine.

"Come on, let's go put those wings to use before we can't. I want to show you a few things."

I set her back on the floor but refuse to let her out of my reach as we walk through the rooms. Now that I'm not starving, I can see that someone has carved most of this place out of the inside of the mountain.

"Who made this place?"

"Uncle Ty did. He said it took years, but at the time he had nothing else to do. I believe it's built in front of his old ship, ANDI."

"I need to talk to him about ANDI. I need to see if there is a way to connect him to my ship as the AI on the Traveler is unresponsive. I am hoping grandfather will have an idea on how to override her and replace her with ANDI. That is if his older programming can even understand the new ship."

"Come on, we'll worry about saving us all in a few hours. I want you to myself for just a little bit because I believe we'll be extremely busy before long. When you were watching TV on those satellites in space, was there someplace you wanted to see?"

"Only your face."

CHAPTER 11
KATHERINE

The moment we step outside, he grabs me from behind and launches us into the air. He holds me tightly against him, my back to his chest. I hold my arms out, laughing as RaZ's wings beat loudly behind me.

"I was worried you would be scared but it looks like I have been blessed with a natural adventurer."

"I'm jealous, I want a pair of my own."

"I have had them all of my life, and I have never enjoyed them as much as I am right now."

We glide over the mountain tops. The lush green forest surrounding us is still beautifully untouched by the horrors unfolding across the rest of the planet. I motion for him to land in a grassy valley below us.

RaZ pushes my hair back off my face when we land, his hand gently caressing my face. I have spent multiple days and so many hours worrying and scared that this, or should I say ... HIM ... would all be a big mistake. But the moment I was in his arms, I knew this was exactly where I was supposed to be.

I had already fallen in love with him ... and at the time, he was just a figment of my imagination. Now that he's here, I'm overwhelmed by his mere presence. He starts to say something, and I put my fingers over his lips.

"Stand still, I just want to look at you."

I walk around him slowly, running my hands over his muscular frame. His large wings quiver as I caress them softly. I lean against his back between his wings and rub my nose on his soft skin as I trace the contours of his back. His muscles seem more defined here, showing the strength his body needs to hold up his massive wings. Wings that are so large they are skimming the ground at our feet. Long black hair hangs to the middle of his back, much like my own, except his is coarser in texture. He doesn't say a word, simply stands there as I take my time exploring his body. I make my way to his chest, tracing every dip and line. Multiple scars stretch across his body. I plan on finding out the story behind each one. As I run my hands down his sides, there is no missing his very prominent erection. I move in closer and grab his butt pulling our bodies together.

"Little female, you are playing with fire. I have been alone for years and up until this moment, I thought that was the worst torture. I will not be able to hold back from taking you right here and now if you do not stop. I want our first time to be special, not rushed like two younglings."

"RaZ, I'm not a child. I'm hundreds of years old, and if I have learned anything in all those years, it's that if you want something, you'd better take it. Time is cruel and there is no such thing as the perfect time. Everything works out just the way it's supposed to. I feel like I've waited my whole life to be standing right here, in this moment with you. People say that love at first sight is bullshit. I didn't have an opinion one way or another until now."

His red eyes flash silver and I can see his love for me reflected in them.

"I knew without a doubt you were mine the moment I saw you on that holo screen. It was at that very moment in time that my heart finally started beating. I have no idea what the Lord of Light has planned for us, but I will never be doubtful of his ways again. He brought me here safely through the unknown, to be by your side, and hold you in my arms like this. This feels like a dream and if it is, then do not wake me up. I will gladly stay in this world and this moment with you forever."

I look up at the sky above us.

"RaZ, I have spent multiple nights in my life stargazing. I never knew I was looking for you. Never dreamed that on one of those distant stars was the one person meant solely for me. I don't know who your Lord of Light is, but the next time you pray to him, tell him thank you for me."

Stepping away, I motion for him to follow me. There's a small cove just through the trees that I found years ago. It's one I love coming to when I need a break from the world; this one and the one in between. He has to duck down to get under the branches. His wings are so large that they brush the leaves aside as he walks forward.

He lets out a small whistle. "This is a hidden gem you have here. I do not know if I could even have spotted it from the air. These massive rocks hide this well."

I try to look at this place through his eyes. Two tall cliff walls merge together creating a shaded grassy area between them. Huge trees branch out into a large canopy above us. A small stream runs off to the side, the sound of water trickling down the rocks so very soothing. I've been here so many times that I started bringing things with me. I walk over to one of the many trees lining the cliff wall and pull out a container with a blanket and a few books I've read multiple times.

As I lay the blanket out on the ground, RaZ never moves. He simply stands there watching me as I slowly start sliding my sundress off. I stand before him naked and vulnerable. In all of my years, I have never opened myself up to another like this.

I watch him open and close his fist as he fights to stand there.

"I know this seems forward and rushed, but I have a feeling that our alone time is going to be few and far between for quite some time. I think we should take advantage of every minute now, like it's our last. I don't want to regret not acting on my feelings because someone might say it is too quick and that I'm leading with my emotions rather than my brain. I've been raised in a world full of rules, and there are some prudes who try to say what a woman should or shouldn't do with her body. If you sleep with a guy on the first date, you're a whore and unworthy. If you give your body to a man before marriage you're impure. But for the first time in my life, I don't care. I'm shutting out the rules and the standards only women are supposed to live by and I'm going to take what I want. If you break my heart later, it's all on me.

I want to experience the three C's in life: Choice, Chance, and Change! And I want them all with you. I have no idea what it is about one person in this life that claims your heart and your soul. And I will never understand the pull of love, but I pray we have hundreds of years to figure it all out."

In the blink of an eye, RaZ is inches from me. I can feel the heat radiating off his body as he lovingly cups my cheek. He seems to take a deep breath as I stare up at him. I can tell he is searching for the right words to say.

"I have dreamed of you, and I have made love to you so many times I feel like I already know your body intimately, but my dreams could never fathom or compare to you. There are no words to explain your true beauty. The very sight of you standing here in front of me takes my very breath away." He lowers his head down, rubbing his cheek against mine and I swear I feel the tension leave his body with a single breath. Then he kisses me so gently.

He steps back from me and with the touch of what looks like a button on his pants, they simply disappear. I make myself focus on his face as my eyes instantly want to explore him further. RaZ stretches his wings all the way out, revealing himself fully. I wish I had a way to forever capture the winged God as he stands before me right now. His features are so beautiful that he's hard to look at. I've been all over the world and seen the beauty it has to offer, but there isn't a single thing I can compare him to. His red eyes flash silver ... I notice they seem to do that when he's fighting his emotions. He pulls me near and from the look on his face, I feel like I'm about to be consumed. My body tingles all over as it reacts to the feel of his naked skin upon my own.

I close my eyes and lean my head against his chest, enjoying the feel and smell that is simply RaZ. I smile to myself when I realize the top of my head barely reaches his shoulders. His massive wings wrap around me and for the first time in my life, I let go. I raise my arms up, wrapping them around his neck, pulling him to me. My soul is trying to absorb him and I feel like I can't get close enough.

My body tingles as his claws lightly scratch my back. A shiver runs through me from his gentle caress. A growl leaves his throat as he lifts me up and into his arms. My legs wrap around his waist as his lips capture mine once again. My nipples pebble hard as they are smashed between us. I rub myself on him wantonly. For the first time in my life, I simply let myself feel.

I don't even notice him lowering us to the ground until I feel the cold on my back. He holds himself above me, his wings stretched out above the ground around us, enclosing us in our own little world. He slowly lowers himself, giving me time to adjust to his weight as he settles himself between my legs. I can feel his erection pulsing between us just at my entrance and every time I try to bring him inside me, he moves back, teasing me to the point I can feel my own juices flowing freely between my legs. He releases my mouth only to pepper my face with small kisses. He doesn't leave a single spot untouched as his lips and hands explore my body, playing me like a well-used instrument. I arch up when his lips close around one of my nipples. His other hand drifts down my sides, finally lowering between my legs. The moment he inserts a finger inside me, my legs start shaking. He doesn't move them though, no matter how much I squirm.

When RaZ looks up at me with a smirk on his handsome face, I realize I've been gripping his hair the whole time. I loosen my grip as he slides lower, his long hair now tickling my stomach as he glides further down my body. The moment I feel his breath on my inner thigh I tense up, waiting for the pleasure my body knows is coming. But he shocks me when I feel him nipping at the soft flesh all around my folds. He brushes his cheek against my clit, and it feels like a lightning bolt has hit me as pleasure surges throughout my body.

He doesn't wait another moment. RaZ licks me from top to bottom as he plunges another finger inside of me and my body explodes from the invasion. He doesn't give me a second to recover as his fingers start to piston in and out of me. He sucks on my clit, and the second orgasm has me screaming out his name.

He barely gives me a moment to catch my breath as he makes his way back up my body and recaptures my lips with his own. I can taste myself on his lips as I greedily suck on his tongue. I grab onto his butt bringing him right up to my entrance and before he can back away this time, I raise myself up. But he is onto me and lifts his hips back out of the way.

"Quit teasing me!"

RaZ's laughter lightens my heart. "Patience, my little wanton! I must make sure you are ready for me."

I pout when I think he's lifting himself off me again, but he's simply moved us so that I'm now straddling his lap.

"I think this position may be a little easier the first time. Ride me beautiful, make all my dreams come true."

I don't think twice in my hurry to have him inside of me, so I don't take the time to explore him as I should. I lower myself down and feel his crown break through my lips. The lower I go, the more differences I suddenly encounter. Every inch, I feel another crown or large ring of some sort encompassing him. They feel like they're swelling individually and getting larger, the lower I go. I must stop to take a breath and my legs quiver as I'm overly stimulated.

My clit pulses when he nips my neck gently. He grips my butt, holding me still above him and giving me time to adjust to his size. I have no idea how much more of him I can take. I raise myself back up slowly feeling each rib of his cock catch before it leaves me. This time RaZ moves his hips up and down easing his way in more with each stroke. And just when I think I can't take another centimeter, he bites me hard, making me cum for the third time. My walls spasm around him as he slams the rest of the way in. I can feel my legs sitting on his and I'm so weak I can barely move.

RaZ wraps his arms around me, lowering me up and down gently until I feel like my brain comes back online. When I look up at his beautiful face, his eyes are closed, his teeth are clenched together and I can see how hard it is for him to hold back.

"I won't break, love me RaZ!"

My words must have snapped something inside of him because I find myself being consumed as he launches us up off the ground and into the sky. He never misses a beat as his body molds me into his own personal sex toy. I scream out twice more and when my inner lips grasp him tightly this last time, I finally feel him let go as his very essence is being pumped inside of me.

RaZ lowers us back to the ground, laying me down gently upon the blanket. He lies down beside me, tucking me into his side. Both of our bodies are covered in sweat. My body still trembles with the intensity of what just happened between us. He pulls me close, covering me with one of his wings. I close my eyes and tuck my head against his chest, simply enjoying the feeling of him next to me. We lay there content, neither one of us saying a word for some time. I've never experienced anything like this and I'm in a daze, reliving what had just happened in my head. I had no idea my body could react or respond that way. *If this is what it's like to be abducted by aliens, bring it on!* I giggle as that thought goes through my head.

"What is so funny?"

"Oh, just a little alien, human humor floating through my mind."

CHAPTER 12

RAZ

Raising up on my elbow, I look down at her flushed face. I have never seen anything more beautiful in all my existence. I now understand the look in my father's eyes when he gazes at his Kira. I didn't have a frame of reference for romantic love growing up, since there were just males in our home. We all understood loyalty, brotherhood, and family. But I did not know we were missing the biggest part ... until this very moment.

Females are what make you strive for more. They are the ones that make your dwelling a home and a place of refuge. Their arms provide you with pleasures that any male worth his weight in treasure would give his very life to protect. I have been searching all my life for something; I just had no idea what until now. I push a few stray hairs off her face and she opens her eyes, smiling up at me.

"I dreamed of you when I was on the ship."

"Did you now? Were these dreams sexy in nature?"

I laugh. "No, those were the ones I made up in my mind. I believe I may have dreamed about your youth. If it was not you, the girl had to be a sister. I watched you die ... as a youngling. You were so small, barely knee-high and there was a pale-haired female with you.

You found some pups, but one was more than it seemed ... I could tell by the aura around it. The bite on your hand took your life force, but not the other females, even though she got extremely sick. I even watched them put you in the ground. And then your spirit came to me, showing me so many different things about your life. I believe I may have even seen you reborn to the same pale-headed female. It was like I was walking along with you through different parts of your life."

She looks up at me, shocked.

"My father also relived pieces of my mother's life. I have never heard of anyone else ever doing that. RaZ, those weren't dreams, everything you saw happened. When I died the first time, I was in the in-between. There were times I wanted to fade as the others had before me, but I had to stay and watch over Emma. That's the girl you saw, and that girl is my mother ... in this life anyhow.

"I was in the afterlife when I simply happened upon Victoria by mistake; her mind was searching for peace as her body was being destroyed by one of the originals, an ancient that came from your world. I held her soul until I found a way to get Tyberius to her. She was moments from actual death, and you know, vampires are hard to kill. I try not to think about the horrors she experienced as she hung in those chains for years."

"Who did that to her?"

"Marcus, one of the original Ancients."

I sit up, startled by what she just told me.

"There is no way he did this ... Marcus was a warrior. He was an honored Elite in our world!"

"He was a monster! I'm sorry; I know some of what you are going to hear will be upsetting. Uncle Ty will know the exact details of what happened between them. I think this is something you should talk to him about when we get back. But as for me, I am pieces of them all. I'm part Hellhound like my mother, part vampire like my father. But mostly, I speak to the dead, or I should say, I can hold onto the spirits of the dead. I spent hundreds of years becoming strong in the in-between when the Hellhound venom killed me as a child.

I taught myself how to recapture the spirits of those who passed. And many times, I grabbed them only to replant them into a child or another pup being born. This is how I was reborn: the moment Emma became pregnant, I implanted myself into the new cells forming inside her. I reincarnated myself, as I have had to do for Ghost and quite a few of my other pups for years now. The nice thing is once you mature, you retain the memories of your former life. This can be a curse or a blessing depending on how you perceive it though. Most human minds can't cope with so much knowledge. I learned this the hard way early on."

I caress her cheek, mesmerized by the creature lying before me.

"That helps to explain some of the things I saw. Your abilities are amazing and yet terrifying, Katherine. I do not know if things will be the same for you on Darverius and this concerns me."

"Ty and Father are worried about that too since none of us know how my body will react once we leave the atmosphere."

She looks away from me for a moment and I swear it is like I have her body, but her spirit has left. Moments later, I see her eyebrows drop and she looks worried.

"We have to get dressed. Something is wrong around us ... The spirits are telling us to hurry."

I do not question her. I simply jerk her up off the ground. With a thought, my pants reappear and the second her garment settles around her hips, I have us in the air. And not a moment too soon, as the ground we had just been laying on starts to tremble aggressively. I see one of the large trees that had been protecting us only moments earlier crash to the ground. It would have landed directly on us if she had not been warned. I turn us slowly in the air, watching as the land below buckles and cracks from forces unseen beneath it.

"We should head back and make sure everyone is ok. I can feel Dad, but Mom is blocking me for some reason."

As I fly us back toward Grandfather's dwelling, I can see the destruction creeping this way. Far away, fires light up the night sky as dark, heavy smoke lifts high into the lingering clouds. Lightning flashes brightly in front of us as the winds start to pick back up. We no sooner make it through the large door of the grandfather's home when the hail and slashing rain start. Grandfather meets us at the doorway with another male. I stumble in my tracks when I realize it's the male I saw in her dreams ... The one that's just like me.

Katherine runs to him, hugging him tightly.

"RaZ, I would like you to meet my father, Lucas."

It takes a tic for me to find my voice, as I feel like a youngling being severely judged as he looks me up and down.

"Sir, it is a pleasure."

The male glances down at Katherine, and you can plainly see his love for her on his face.

"Your mother isn't feeling well; she is in the parlor with Vic ... you go on. We have things to discuss."

He pulls her close for another hug. I see red tears in his eyes as he lays his head on top of hers for a moment. She pulls away and reaches up to kiss him on the cheek.

"Love you, daddy."

"Love you too, baby girl. Now go on and visit with the girls. I promise I won't hurt RaZ too bad. I forgot my shotgun at the manor!"

Katherine smiles at me right before she walks away, and it takes everything I have not to call her back. I feel his eyes on me, judging me as I stand there watching her. I have no idea why I am letting this male ruffle my wings.

Grandfather touches my shoulder gently.

"RaZ, we have much to speak of, but before we get started, Lucas has asked for a moment of your time. I will be in the lower holding chamber when you two get done."

Katherine's father and I stand eye to eye. Just as I start to speak, he holds his hand up stopping me.

"I have a lot of respect for you, young man. It takes an extraordinarily strong male to pick up and leave everything he knows for the unknown and that's what you did. I understand that you've traveled a great distance to save your grandfather and my daughter. Since my grumpy old ass hates technology, I can't even fathom what you've done, but I personally thank you for it. Your space travel is beyond my comprehension and until you walked in this room, a creature from the stars ... I didn't honestly believe all the stories Ty told. I knew he came from somewhere, but my mind simply couldn't believe the words he spoke.

Since they lost contact again right after that first transmission, they weren't sure of the time frame that one, or many of you, might take to get here. I will say I was hesitant at first, unwilling to get my hopes up that someone would arrive in time to save my child. Even though she has been grown for centuries, every time I see her ... well she will always be my little girl.

When Kat said she could feel you getting closer, I dreaded the day you would arrive almost as much as I wished you were already here. You are going to take one of my most treasured blessings away. And being her father, I'm having a hard time letting her go. I want what all parents want: to watch her fall in love and have little ones of her own. To have grandchildren I could spoil. I wanted to share her life until the day the gods took me from this place. But that's not in the cards and as hard as this is for me, I must hand her over to you with a full heart. I pray that you will do everything in your power to keep her happy and safe, as I won't be there to pick her up if she falls."

I can feel his despair like it's my own.

"Why are you acting like you won't be there? I have plenty of room on the Traveler for all of us."

"My Emma won't make it if she is separated from the Earth, and I won't make it without her. I'm a man, or should I say a father, torn. It took some time for my Emma to finally convince me that you are my Kat's soulmate. She woke up one night and sat straight up in bed, tears flowing down her face. She said she saw Kat in another place, a world full of strange colors. In her dream it looked like Kat was flying, but as she looked closer, she could see someone was holding her. The man's wings were stretched out wide and she could hear Kat laughing as you two soared through the skies. Now that you stand before me with those massive things on your back, it's obvious now that you were the one holding her. Emma said she had never seen such joy on Kat's face before. And we both knew right then that she would leave us for this world of colors. I want you to know that if it weren't for the very Earth beneath us being on the verge of destruction, I would fight to keep her here, even if I had to destroy you to do it!"

He turns from me, running his hands through his hair, red tears streaking down his cheeks.

"But I want her to live. So, son with that said, I may not be in your world physically, but I will watch over you both from the heavens. If you ever hurt her, death will not stop my reckoning!"

"Sir, if I may speak freely. The moment I laid eyes upon her, my whole world changed. I will do everything in my power to make her happy. We have so many unknowns to conquer before us. And because of that, as the sands of time are forever shifting, I am determined to cherish every minute I have with her. We can take nothing for granted, but I vow to you male to male, she is the only reason for my next breath. I will treasure her always."

He wipes the tears from his face and pats me on the shoulder.

"That's all a dad can ask, son. Come on now ... T has questions and I'm eager to help in any way I can to see you guys leave safely from here."

CHAPTER 13

KATHERINE

"Mom, do you think it's safe to leave RaZ with Dad? I mean daddy can be pretty intense at times."

"Oh, I'm sure your man will survive whatever your father throws at him. You know he needs to threaten him a little bit, that's what dads are supposed to do. So, speaking of your man ... is he as impressive as you thought he would be?"

My jaw drops when she wiggles her eyebrows suggestively.

"Mother, shame on you. There is no way you just asked me that question!"

"Well, Kat, the man has traveled for years to get here. There are only so many ways to play with that thing ... it's a wonder he didn't blow your head off."

"Mother! What in the world?"

I shake my head and turn away as I know my face is blood red. Lord, I never know what is going to come out of her mouth. I pace the room, chewing on my fingernails. I didn't tell RaZ this, but something big is coming. It's like I can feel the Earth holding its breath and when it exhales, we're all doomed.

Aunt Vic walks up behind me and gently rubs my back.

"Now Katherine, don't be bashful, we're all adults here. There's nothing wrong with a little kiss and tell, so spill it! Your mother and I have both lived a long time, and we could use some new gossip."

"I'm not telling either one of you anything, you old perverts."

Vic puts her hand over her heart, acting as if she's heartbroken.

"Bummer! I will say, it took quite a bit of convincing on my end to keep your mother from racing out or sending one of the pups after you two. Especially after Ty came in and said you two were leaving for a little bit. Fortunately for me, I just happened to be standing at this very window when I suddenly saw two very large wings. Those wings were attached to a very nice ass and it was flying away with you. For a moment I was almost jealous, then I got over it."

Mom and Vic both crack up laughing at the look on my face.

"You two need to quit! My face will stay permanently red at this rate."

I point at Aunt Victoria. "And you're not supposed to be looking at his ass!"

"Sweetie, I may be old, but I'm not dead. And that young man was fine, at least from this angle anyway."

The laughter in the room stops suddenly when Mom stands up. I've seen that look on her face many times before and it's never good.

"Mom?"

"The storm has gotten worse to the west, and more of my babies have been taken. Wait … I'm not sure … But … the presence … it feels familiar, almost like Rage. It's getting closer … We must find her!" She starts walking away.

"Mom, stop! We barely made it back to the front door before it started hailing out, and the stones are so large they would beat us to death in seconds. We can't go out there right now."

She's staring off, looking at nothing.

"It's small, but its soul is strong. She's the last of her kind, an alpha female. Oh! She's Rage's daughter. I'm trying to look through her eyes, but she keeps tucking her head in. She's hiding up against what looks like human skin. She's too young to show me what's around her. But the rain is hurting her skin. I can see a hand pull her head closer; someone is trying to protect her."

A yelp leaves my mother's lips as she feels and experiences everything the Hellhound pup is going through.

"She's falling … Wait a minute, small human hands grab her just in time. She's being jostled around. I can see little feet running barefoot through the mud, and hailstones are laying all over the ground around them. She's trying to wiggle free because she's scared and wants to go back to her mother. I have to tell her to stay with the human. Her mommy is gone … I felt her and her other babies leave. I didn't know the runt survived."

I'm so focused on Mom I almost miss the sound. A faint knock on the door has all three of us running toward it. Mom somehow reaches it first and just about jerks it off its hinges. Standing in the rain is a little boy, holding a small black pup in his arms.

"My mommy told me to run to the big door in the mountain. That you would help us."

The pup whines in his arms, squirming to get loose. He pets the pup lovingly, bouncing her gently, trying to calm her like you would a baby.

"No Raven, be good," We hear him say gently.

I pull the child in out of the rain. Victoria appears with towels in her arms, and we both start to dry him off. Mom starts to reach for the pup, but he just hugs it tighter. Tears flow down his face as his little body shakes all over.

I gently wipe his face off. He has bruises all over him, from the hail and Lord knows what else.

"Sweetie ... who is your mommy? Where did you come from?"

"My mommy's name is Joann."

The moment he says her name he starts to cry harder.

"We have been walking for days, hiding from the bad people. Mamaw told her that there was a safe place in the hills, and if we found the big door in the mountain, we would be protected. She was supposed to tell you that she is Mary's great-granddaughter. She told me this story over and over so that I wouldn't forget it if we got separated.

I tried hard to keep up with mommy, but I was so tired. My feet hurt and my belly kept growling, but mommy kept encouraging me to keep going. She was excited about all the adventures we were going to go on and all the good food that was waiting for us. Suddenly, the ground started shaking all around us and all the big trees started falling. I heard mommy yell my name out a second before she pushed me out of the way, but she didn't move in time. I heard her scream behind me as one of the trees crashed.

I picked myself up off the ground and called out to her, but she didn't answer. It took me a minute to climb through the branches and that's when I saw her. The tree had pinned her under it. Mommy was having a hard time breathing, and she had blood on her lips. I tried to pull her out, but the tree was too heavy. When I started to dig in the dirt around her, Mommy grabbed my arm to make me stop.

Mommy got her serious face when she knew I wasn't going to be able to get her out. She made me leave even though I didn't want to, because the woods are really scary when you're by yourself. She made me promise not to look back and to keep running until I found the big door in the mountain. I ran as hard and fast as I could and now that I've found you, I need to go back and get mommy. She'll be scared out there all alone. Here, please take Raven."

He tries to hand the puppy to me.

"I had to slow down for a minute because my side was hurting, but I kept walking. Then I heard something whining. When I found her, she was hiding under some brush. I had to crawl under it to get her out. I could tell that she was cold and scared out there all by herself. I looked for her mommy too, but I couldn't find her anywhere. So, I decided I would bring her with me because she was too small to be out there all alone, so please take her and keep her safe until I get back!"

I catch his arm gently. He's practically sobbing; each word coming out of his mouth is tearing my heart out.

"No sweetie ... you need to stay here. Let's get you cleaned up and in some dry clothes. Your mommy wouldn't want someone as brave as you are to get sick, especially since you found your way here all on your own. Let me send one of the guys out to see if they can find her. Raven needs you here with her right now; she may get scared if you leave."

"But they don't know where she is. Mom needs me!"

I wipe the snot off his nose and try my best to dry his tears. I can tell he's about to collapse. Not only is he extremely thin, but his body is cold and exhausted.

"Lord, you are such a brave child. What's your name, honey?"

"Danny, my name is Danny."

He no more than says his name as he simply starts to wilt in front of me. I grab him just in time, only to notice the multiple scratches all over his arms. Raven's eyes flash red as she jumps out of his arms. Mom catches her before she can slip away.

I look up at Mom; we both know his chances are slim now that a Hellhound has scratched him. To this day the only survivor I know of is standing beside me with a wet puppy in her arms. My own mother.

Victoria gently takes him out of my arms, his little legs dangling limply as she walks carefully toward one of the bedrooms.

"Let's make him as comfortable as possible. To be so young and to have lost so much, let's see if we can make his last hours peaceful at least."

Mom turns away with the pup still in her arms. I can see her whispering to it and instead of her taking the little thing to Ghost or Glory, she starts to follow Aunt Vic down the hallway.

"Where are you taking her, Mom?"

"She wants to stay with him. She told me he was hers."

I walk in the room last, just as Victoria is laying him down. Raven wiggles until Mom sets her down on the bed with him. Then she tucks herself into his side, and even though I can tell the pup is exhausted, she never closes her eyes; she simply watches us as we move around the room.

Victoria puts the back of her hand on his forehead.

"Katherine, can you get a read on him? Do you know if it will take long for his spirit to leave his body? He already has a slight temperature."

I sit down on the bed next to him after Vic and Mom strip his wet clothes off. I pull the blanket up and move Raven over for a second until I can tuck him in comfortably. She growls at me, and I can't help but smile as she isn't much bigger than my hand. Too bad she has attached herself to the boy as it will be hard for her when she realizes she was the one who took his life.

I close my eyes and rest my hand on his chest. At first, I don't see anything, but then I see a woman's face. Her eyes are the same as the boys'. She hovers over his body, her spirit confused as she tries to hold on to him. This must be his mother. I walk into the in-between and approach her slowly. All new spirits startle easily, and I want her to know it's okay for her to let go. He'll be joining her soon.

Communicating with the dead isn't the same as having a conversation with the living. You really don't talk; it's more about emotions and gestures. The woman still doesn't realize she's dead and that makes it harder.

I motion to the boy and then back to myself, trying to show her that he's safe for now. At first, she just hovers closer to him. Even dead, she's trying to protect him. I glide toward her, touching her arm gently. Once I get her mind to allow me to, I show her the events that have happened once he left her sight. At the very last moment I pull back, as I don't want her to see her son's death coming. Her spirit starts to fade once I show her that he's safe.

She moves directly over him once more and I take her hand in mine so that she can touch him one last time. I fight the tears in my eyes. Even though I didn't know her personally, I can still feel her love for him. Life can be so unfair sometimes. I pull her hand back and gently push her spirit toward the light beckoning to her. Her eyes never leave the boy, until she is no more.

I come back to myself slowly. No matter how many times I walk and interact in the afterlife, certain things still tear at my heart. I feel Victoria's comforting hand on my back as the three of us stand above the child lying in the bed in front of us. No wonder anger and destruction follow so many of them as their young minds don't know how to cope any other way. I'm having a hard time dealing with the possible loss of my parents and I'm an adult.

Raven moves around on the bed as she becomes more comfortable with us. She rolls over onto her back, her stomach showing. Mom reaches down and gently rubs her belly.

"Mom, is his fever going up?"

"No, he seems calm and content at the moment. I see no signs of infection, and I wish I had looked at his scratches closer because they really don't look as bad as they did."

"How old do you think he is?"

"I would say six, maybe seven ... can't be much more than that. Poor little thing is so scrawny you can see every bone in his body."

Victoria sits down on the end of the bed. The storm outside seems to be intensifying, as you can hear things hitting the side of the mountain. None of us says a word; we simply sit there together, praying that the scratches on his little body are something else and that he opens his eyes.

CHAPTER 14
RAZ

I follow Katherine's father down a set of steps that have been carved out of the rock beneath our feet. I know I must stay focused on getting all of us out of here, but what I really want to do is grab Katherine and tuck us into someplace private for a couple hundred years. The steps open up into a huge room. A room that takes my mind a tic to comprehend. It's part of a spaceship. Questions begin flooding my brain.

"Frack! Is this part of the ship you were in when it crashed? How did you do this? How did you survive? What exactly happened for you to crash here?"

Grandfather's voice carries throughout the room.

"To make a long story short, we left Darverius on a routine flight. One minute we were all talking about the upcoming conference and the next it seemed like we woke up here. ANDI had been momentarily knocked offline when the wormhole grabbed us. So, our ship was simply floating aimlessly after we were slung into this solar system. Earth's gravity was so strong at the time that the moment our ship hit its surrounding atmosphere, its pulled us down and we crashed right here.

We were never able to access the main control room after the crash. So, we assumed that anyone who had been in there perished. It didn't take long for the rest of us to begin starving as we only had a limited supply of Blood Beets with us. Marcus was the first to leave looking for food. He brought back a little of everything ... only for our bodies to reject any substance we tried to consume. I have no idea exactly how long he looked, but I know we were only days from perishing.

Marcus accidentally stumbled upon an injured man. The wagon he had been on had turned over and the man was bleeding badly. Marcus went to help move the wagon off him when he smelled the blood. All I know is that he attacked the man, draining him dry. We were amazed when he simply appeared in front of Seamus and I. He looked so healthy that it was like he was glowing from the inside out.

We all became monsters that day. The more we consumed the more we changed inside and out. The blood enhanced everything, from our appearance to our speed and strength. But it all came with a cost. We became the monsters in the storybooks, the urban legends ... The thing mothers threatened their children with if they misbehaved ... the boogeyman. It didn't take long for the humans to recognize us as the predators we were, especially when their loved ones started going missing. We had to start glamouring ourselves and then had to learn to hide in plain sight.

Marcus lived for the chaos; he consumed so much blood that he became deformed. He seized communities and simply took anything he wanted, including their women, their children, and their wealth. Seamus went in a completely different direction as he was fascinated with the small humans around us. He fell in love with a beautiful woman. He hid what he was from her for years until a carriage accident resulted in her being gravely injured. She was moments from dying in his arms when he did something that I felt was unforgivable at the time. Now that I have Victoria, I realize I would have done the same in his shoes. Seamus was the first to change a human into one of us. Their union also showed us that we could reproduce with humans. Lucas is his oldest son and my Victoria is his only sister. When Lucas was born, we realized that our children would inherit our afflictions and the need for blood, and so would their children. A vicious chain that never ended with each generation born.

Because of this, I refused to mate with anyone. I would not be part of a line of monsters who invaded and destroyed this planet. It went against everything I stood for. I didn't want to kill another to survive, and the taste of their deaths was tearing me apart.

One night it all changed for me. I had waited too long to feed. Out of desperation, I tore a man's throat out. When my bloodlust had lessened, I was horrified when I looked up, and I saw his young daughter standing in the doorway watching. Her eyes had filled with tears as she sobbed her father's name. I didn't know I could do this until afterward, but I managed to erase her mind. I then glamoured myself as her father. I raised her and all of her descendants as my own. But no matter how I tried, in my own mind, I could never atone for the things I had done.

Mary and I never spoke of it, but as she got older, she knew I was something else ... especially when she started to age, and I didn't. I finally learned to feed without killing, but it still disgusted me. I hated that my life depended on me taking some of another's life force.

Late one evening, I went to the smokehouse where Mary was butchering a hog to tell her I would be back in the morning. I was weak and had practically starved myself. I knew if I waited much longer, everyone I had come to care about would be in danger.

Mary had drained the blood from the animal and placed it on top of the table in a pitcher, with a small glass sitting beside it. She simply motioned for me to take a seat and handed me the glass. Then she just walked out of the shed as if nothing odd had happened. I was hesitant at first. I was scared the animal blood would make me sick, but I was at the point where I no longer cared.

Mary saved many lives that day as I learned that animal blood could sustain me. Now, it isn't as fulfilling as human blood and I do have to consume more, but as you can see, I am quite healthy. I don't know if Mary's memories ever truly returned, as we never spoke of that day again. All I know is that she made it a point, from that day on, to always have fresh blood available.

Today, I still wear Mary's father's glamor as I can no longer stand the sight of my own skin. I have not aged since we crashed here, so my original appearance simply reminds me of my true barbaric nature.

Lucas, unknowingly until this moment, has employed Mary's descendants for centuries at his manor. I mourn her death to this day because I raised her as my own. The moment I laid her in the ground, I separated myself from the others, including Seamus and Marcus. Lucas and his siblings only knew me as a rumor.

I have spent every waking moment since trying to make amends for the things our kind was doing to others. For hundreds of years, I never left this very dwelling, consumed with finding a way to return home to Darverius and DaR. RaZ, there are no words to express my gratitude for your sacrifice and the devotion it took for you to get here. I know I wasn't your main reason for coming, and even if I don't make it off this rock, I will do everything in my power to get you and Katherine out of here safely.

Now, I have no idea how we are going to sustain all of us on your ship. I have enough blood in this room to last us a year. Unfortunately, now that I understand the trip is much longer than that, I'm truly at a loss as to how to feed all of us for such a long period. We have so much to discuss..."

"Wait a minute ... before we get into the discussion of the trip, where are Marcus and Seamus now? And what happened to everyone else that was on your ship?"

Grandfather looks away from me. I can tell he is struggling with what he is about to tell me.

"I'm the last survivor, RaZ. Marcus and Seamus are dead. I may not have agreed with their ways, but they were the last ties I had to Darverius. Vlad, Radul, and Cassius were in the main cabin of the ship, which was destroyed when we crashed. Alaric's body was never found and there was absolutely no evidence that he was ever with us. He was sitting right next to me, and I can even vaguely remember us talking, but it was like he simply disappeared. We never found a single trace of him. I have so many things to share with you, RaZ. But the main priority is getting us off this planet."

"How long do you think we have?"

"Days at the most."

"Frack, I was hoping for more time. The AI on the Traveler has disconnected itself and the main ship is offline. I am not even sure if the ship needs repairs, or if I can get the other shuttle down here without one of you going up with me to fly it back. With that being said, I am going to assume none of you have any flight experience." They both shake their heads no, but grandfather has a large smile on his face when he speaks.

"I may not have flight experience, but I think I have something that can help us. I can see your mind already working from here. Come on over, RaZ, and I will introduce you to what's left of ANDI. He's the sole reason I remained sane all these years."

"Hello Master RaZ, it's a pleasure to meet you."

My wings flutter behind me when a voice suddenly fills the room.

"I thought ANDI was on the brink of shutting down and that was why all of the signals were on repeat and broadcasting in spurts?"

"ANDI is simply working off a weak computer system at the moment. I have his main programming saved on what the humans call a flash drive. He isn't powerful enough to do anything long-distance now. What I have running here in the mountain isn't nearly as powerful as what I had before the Earth started collapsing. Because the main power core was in our original ship, when it stopped functioning, I almost lost him."

"Do you have a way to transport him?"

"Absolutely, but we have no way of knowing if he can adapt to the programming on your ship."

"There is only one way to find out! If we can get the Traveler back online, it would sure increase our chances of making it off this rock with more than a few months' worth of supplies. My shuttle is hovering above us right now if you think it is worth pursuing."

"Call it down son, and let's hope ANDI has a few more tricks up his invisible sleeves."

I turn at the sound of footsteps coming our way. Grandfather's wife sticks her head in the doorway.

"Ty, you need to come here, we may have a potential problem."

No one says a word as we all simply follow her out of the room and through the maze of corridors carved into this mountain haven.

I can sense Katherine's distress before I step through the door. I immediately go to her side, my wings wrapping around her and pulling her close. Grandfather sits down on the bed in the middle of the room.

"Where did he come from?"

Grandfather's wife speaks up, "Mary sent him and his mother to us. Unfortunately, the mother was crushed by a falling tree. She survived long enough to make him promise he wouldn't stop until he found us."

I watch as grandfather looks up at Katherine. "You know the mother has perished?"

"Yes, I helped her spirit move on, as she was still searching for him in the in-between."

He lowers his head, shaking it sadly. "Why is he unresponsive?"

A woman I have not seen before moves the blanket aside, revealing the scratches on his arms. A small black pup crawls out of the covers and pushes the woman's hand away, a low growl rumbles from its throat as it looks around the room.

Grandfather tries to pick the pup up only for it to swat at him.

"Is this pup what I think it is?"

"Yes, she's an alpha female Hellhound and the last of Rage's descendants. Unfortunately, she has attached herself to the boy."

I watch grandfather rub his hands down the boy's arms shaking his head.

"Is there anything we can do for him? He is also the last of his kind if his mother is gone; the last of my Mary's descendants. Mary will stalk me from the grave if she thinks I'm letting one of her own suffer. He's too young to turn, and I will not be the one to destroy him."

I watch Victoria sit down on the other side of the young male. I can tell by the look in her eyes she's going to do anything to make sure the youngling survives.

"The pup's poison seems to be affecting him differently. Emma says it may be because she's so small that her venom isn't as strong. Although most humans would have died by now either way. The fact that he's still alive says something about their bond. Time will tell whether he survives, but we need to be prepared to take him with us if he does. I will not leave him behind, Ty!"

I watch grandfather reach over and pull her toward him, kissing her on the forehead. "Nor will I, Victoria."

He stands up suddenly, "Come RaZ, we have a family to save and time is of the essence."

I put a finger under Katherine's chin and raise her face up to mine, kissing her gently. "I will be back."

"You'd better."

CHAPTER 15
RAZ

I signal for the shuttle to land at my current location as grandfather and I watch the clouds part as it lowers through them.

"That's a nice little gadget you have there." He motions towards the personal comm on my wrist.

"It is one of many things SoL has invented. It has a limited range and power source and unfortunately, it will only control one shuttle at a time. There is a tracking device inside of it and father gets extremely angry if we do not constantly wear them."

"Who is this SoL to you ... another commander?"

"He is my brother; actually, one of twenty-two sons. The look on your face right now is priceless, as your humans would say. It is a long story and we will have plenty of time on the shuttle to talk about all the males eagerly awaiting your return."

The shuttle lands quietly in front of us. "Come on, let me show you what this female is made of."

We enter the small shuttle, and I motion for him to take the seat next to mine. Once the cabin pressurizes, we lift off the ground, rising slowly. I lower the viewers just as we break through the cloud cover. You can see the decimation getting closer to the mountainside where Grandfather has built his home. Neither of us says a thing as we look out over the destruction that seems to be headed our way. With a flick of my wrist, I shoot us through the atmosphere and toward the Traveler. I look over at grandfather and even though he is pinned to the seat, he has a huge smile on his face. He lets out a "Woo hoo!" and his glamor slips, so for a tic, it is like looking at my own father's smile. Once we level out, he is like a youngling staring out the window at the wonders surrounding us.

"I had given up on the dream that I would ever get to see the stars like this again. The day I saw DaR on the other side of that screen ...Well, I honestly thought that if the Lord of Light took me right then, it was ok. After all, he had answered my prayers to see him once more, but this is so much more than I deserve."

I signal the Traveler to open the outward dock and hold my breath, as I am not sure that it will respond. With the AI offline, I have no way to issue some of the most basic commands. I land the shuttle and the bay doors close behind us. I watch for the atmospheric light to turn green before I open the shuttle door. As soon as the area is secured, I step out, heading toward the control center, until the lack of footsteps behind me makes me stop. I walk back to the shuttle bay, only to find Grandfather standing there, looking around.

"If you think this is impressive, wait until you see the rest of her. The Traveler is a piece of artwork floating in space."

"I know I have been gone a long time, but I'm really feeling my age right now. Lead on, youngling. I'm right behind you. I really hope we can find a way to merge ANDI with the ship's interface. Now that I've seen your ship I'm truly worried, as our ship was nothing like this."

We both enter the main control area, and I reach under the console, showing Grandfather the homemade plug I made to hook up the satellites.

"Well son, here goes nothing. Do you want to do the honors? I don't know if I can willingly plug ANDI into this knowing it may be the last time he's here."

"Are you sure?"

"Yes, he's our best option at this point."

I slip ANDI's drive into the plug and step back. After a few seconds when nothing happens, I start to remove him. I have not even touched the plug before the lights start flashing all around us. The main control panel flickers off and on, then all the lights go off completely and I feel the whole ship power down. Oxygen masks fall out of the ceiling, and I must grab onto the chair in front of me to keep from hitting the ceiling as we lose all life support and atmosphere inside the ship.

The Traveler suddenly starts to tilt sideways as the Earth's gravity starts to pull us closer. My first thoughts were of Katherine and how I have already failed her. My mind starts thinking of a way out of this ship. I grab my mask and detach it from the ceiling hoping it has enough oxygen in it to make it to the shuttle. If we can get there, we may be able to break through the loading dock doors. I motion for Grandfather to follow me, and just as he reaches up for his mask, I feel the Traveler shudder, then her main engines fire. Cool air brushes my face as the gravity is reinstated. I take my mask off and take a deep breath.

"Sorry about that gentlemen, but the Traveler was playing hard to get. The old girl just needed a firm hand. All is well now. It may take me a few days to figure out all these new features, but I will be prepared before you are all ready to depart. The Traveler is a fine machine Master RaZ, and I am honored that you are allowing me to command her."

Grandfather plops back down on his seat.

"Damnit, ANDI, I saw the last couple thousand years pass before my eyes. I'm too old for you to be pulling stunts like that!"

When ANDI just laughs, I wonder for a minute if plugging him in was the smartest thing to do.

"ANDI, do you believe you will be compatible with the Traveler's advanced systems?"

"Master RaZ, they have a saying on Earth ... you can still teach some old dogs new tricks. I've got this."

"Is the other AI still in the main interface?"

"Not that I can detect any signs of ... no."

"Can you tell if the ship has sustained any damage?"

"I'm running a full diagnostic panel right now. Ohhh ... well, lucky us, we have repair bots! Boy, I sure could have used these little beauties on Earth. That old rust bucket of mine just might have been salvageable at one time, if I'd had access to these."

"Are there any parts on your original ship that can be salvaged? Maybe something that could help us with food storage?"

"Possibly, after a few small repairs are made to the Traveler's hull. I will send the repair bots to the surface to see if my original cargo hold can be attached to her somehow. That would provide a non-atmospherically controlled environment for items that can withstand the extreme temperatures of space, and it would also free up more room on the main ship.

I believe that would also make Mistress Victoria happy as she could load the cargo hold with clothing and select furniture. We originally believed that the ladies would have to leave most comforts behind. They have been trying to downsize the important things they were going to try to bring along for quite some time now.

"If my calculations are right, I believe if both shuttles are connected to the cargo hold, they will be strong enough to break through the Earth's atmosphere. I will have a plan in place on how we can tow it without it being a drag on the main engines as soon as possible."

"Master RaZ, is there a way for me to speak to you directly from up here?"

"Yes, you can message me through my personal comm at all times."

"Fabulous, now I have work to do and you two need to return to Earth and prepare the items to load into the cargo bay. I will notify you, Master RaZ, as soon as the repair bots are on their way to your location. Also, Ty, there are two cryo-stasis units available in the Med Bay. You should tell Mistress Victoria about them and list their features as this may help her with the anxiety she has been hiding from you. You know she is terrified of dark, cold places and that's all space is to her. She could rest for the majority of the trip, if not the entire trip. She would just go to sleep after we leave Earth, and you wouldn't have to wake her up until we have landed on Darverius."

Grandfather runs his hand across the console, "Damn, ANDI, it's good to have you back, old friend."

"Our journey isn't over yet Ty, and the stars are calling our name. We have many more adventures ahead of us."

CHAPTER 16

KATHERINE

I stand here watching the sky through the window, awaiting RaZ's return. We have been so busy with everything going on that I haven't had an extra moment with him. The few minutes we stole when he first arrived almost feel like I dreamed them.

Ever since he left with Uncle Ty, I've felt uneasy. I think so much has occurred in such a short amount of time that I'm simply expecting something bad to happen. The rain and hail have stopped for now and the sun is out. If you didn't know about the mass destruction that was happening all over the world, you'd think it was just simply another pretty spring day.

Mom and Victoria have taken turns sitting with Danny. He's still lying there on the bed resting peacefully. But if things don't change for him soon, it won't take long for his body to start to deteriorate, as none of us can make it without food for long. The little Hellhound pup has become more comfortable around all of us and is now playing tug of war with Mom on the bed.

Walking away from the window, I run my hand across Mom's back as I walk out of the room. I don't know where I'm headed, but I can't stand here another minute. I make my way to the bedroom I have been using while staying here and look around at the mess I've made going through all my stuff.

The few things I refuse to part with are my pictures of mom and dad, and a small jewelry box full of "pretties". I'll find a way to stuff those things into the final bag I'm going to take with me one way or another. I've gone through everything here multiple times, putting things in and then taking them back out. I don't have a huge collection of important items, but I've lived for hundreds of years and I'm a normal female. I have things I don't want to part with, but I would throw it all away if I could just get mom and dad to go with me. My mind is so troubled, I don't hear Dad walk into the room, and I can't help the small screech that leaves my throat when I hear the voice behind me.

"You still trying to figure out what to take or are you hiding?"

"Shit, you scared the crap out of me and yeah, you caught me. I think I'm doing a little bit of both, Dad. Actually, I was just thinking about you and mom. Dad, we don't have long; I can feel it."

"I know, I can feel it too ... that's why I've come to help you. Since your mom and I aren't leaving with you, there will be more room for you to take your stuff. So, let's get as much of this room as possible packed or into a bag. I'm sure RaZ and Ty will be returning soon and everything we can get done now will be one less thing ... Especially if things get rough quickly."

I sit down on the end of the bed, fighting the tears that want to spill down my face. "I don't know how you can talk about this like it's no big deal, Dad, because it's tearing me apart! I mean you're either going to die here or out there. I understand your worries about Mom, but if this were me, wouldn't you tell me that you wanted every second of every minute we could possibly have together? Please, don't make me get on that ship without you!"

"I understand what you're saying Kat and I don't want you to think for a moment that this is what we want either. There are so many unknowns coming our way, but your mother has seemed stronger these last few days. I don't know if it's the boy or the Hellhound pup, but the moment they arrived she was acting more like her old self. I will talk to your mother but either way, we need to get you ready."

Voices in the hallway echo down the passage. "RaZ, we're in here," Dad yells out before I can say a word.

I smile as I watch RaZ duck as he walks into the bedroom. His wings are so large they almost hit the doorframe. I immediately run to him, wrapping my arms around his waist.

He loosens my arms and picks me up off the ground, bringing me eye-level so my feet dangle in the air like a little kid.

"I see that you missed me." Laughing, he kisses me on the nose before he sets me back down.

I stick my tongue out at him and act like I'm pouting. "Yeah, maybe just a little bit, but I have no idea why. I was so uneasy about you heading back up there, but it's ok now that you're back and in one piece. Did you get ANDI working?"

"He is a work in progress, but yes, I believe once he gets a feel for the old girl, as he calls the Traveler, he will be a true asset. I see that you are packing ... Don't worry about picking only certain things, since we are going to hook up the old cargo hold of ANDI's and that should provide plenty of room for all your stuff."

"Really, that's the best news I have heard all day. After all, girls require lots of accessories and I was at a loss on what to take."

Dad clears his throat, and we both turn to look at him.

"RaZ now that you have returned, I'll let you two take care of this. I will see if Ty needs help as I know he will want to take every book he has ever bought with him. And you better hope that cargo hold is huge, because it will need to be if you haven't ever seen Victoria's closet."

RaZ laughs. "We should have plenty of room with both ships, sir. I also wanted you to know that there is also a full medical bay on the Traveler, something for you to think about."

"I will take that into consideration."

"Dad, you promised you would talk to Mom!"

"I'm headed that way now."

We both stand there as Dad leaves the room, and suddenly, I'm at a loss as to what to talk about as RaZ looks around.

"Is this all you have here or is there more somewhere else?"

"Actually, I have a few cases already in the cargo hold. Ty stored a lot of our stuff there when we first arrived."

"That worked out then, so let's get busy getting you packed. Leave out only what you think you will need for the next couple of rotations, I mean days. As soon as we find a way to connect the cargo hold to the shuttles we will be leaving."

"I wish..."

RaZ puts his fingers over my lips stopping what I was about to say. "I know things are not as we wish they were Katherine, but we will have years together on the Traveler so that we can lock the door and enjoy each other. I look forward to long talks and hours of worshiping your body."

"When you put it like that, we need to pack faster!"

The laughter coming from him lightens my heart. I throw one of the bags lying on the floor at him and he snatches it out of the air.

"Where do you want me to start?"

"Pick a drawer, and yes I will need all of that lingerie."

After opening the top drawer, Raz holds up a piece and then looks over at me. "Yes, this drawer is definitely going!"

I turn around and head for the wardrobe with a smile on my face, letting myself be hopeful for the first time in a while.

We made what seemed like a million trips up and down the stairs. Mom, Dad, and Vic made as many as we did as we all maneuvered the items we were carrying down the steep stairway. I almost jumped up and down when I saw Dad actually packing a few of his and Mom's things too.

It felt good to have a plan instead of standing around waiting for something to happen. ANDI just contacted RaZ, and he's sending some kinda 'bot' to help with securing the cargo hold. If things continue, we'll be on the shuttles and heading toward the bigger ship sometime tomorrow.

We worked all through the night, which is one of the nicest things about not being human because all of us can go for days without sleep. Each of us takes turns checking on Danny through the night.

I'm glad to see that at some point he's moved onto his side on his own, but still nothing we've tried has woken him up. Little Raven still refuses to leave his side for more than a minute or two at a time. She runs out the door to pee and runs right back in, clawing at his bed for one of us to pick her up and put her back up there with him.

One good thing is that Danny's fever broke during the night and the scratches on his arms are practically healed. Unfortunately, none of us have any idea what to expect now. I'm making my way back up the steps after taking a load of dresses down for Victoria when RaZ grabs me from behind.

"I think they can manage for a few minutes without us. Do you want to sneak away?"

"You don't have to ask me twice, I'm easy."

He takes the stairs three at a time with his long legs. I can't help but laugh as he runs to the front door when he hears someone calling out his name. He jerks the door open, and within two steps, we launch into the sky.

I know I shouldn't be so trusting, but I know in my heart that RaZ would destroy himself before he would ever willingly hurt me. I feel like I only know bits and pieces of his personality, but this fun playfulness is just what I need right now. He flies us away from the destruction you can see coming in the distance. It's almost like the Earth has been split in two; one side is perfect, the other destroyed. I hold my arms out pretending I'm flying on my own. RaZ dips down fast and I jerk my arms back down, grasping him tightly as his laughter rings out behind me.

I can feel him relax as he glides on the wind currents. The cool air rushing past us pushes me firmly against his warmer body behind me. I can't help but wiggle my butt against him as I can feel his hardened length pulsing against my back. An uncontrollable shiver races down my whole body when he starts kissing the back of my neck.

"Hey, no fair, don't you need to pay attention to where we're going? In case a tree or something jumps out at us. If you take us down, two of us can play this game."

"What if I like the fact that you are completely at my mercy?"

Just as I start to answer him, I hear a large boom coming from above us. What looks like two small meteors breaks through the cloud cover and is heading straight towards us.

"Katherine, can you hit the red button on top of my comm unit? I would, but I'm not comfortable holding you with one arm in these winds."

"Yeah, keep both hands on the girl!" It takes me a second to figure out what he's talking about, but I must have gotten it right because ANDI's voice immediately sounds like it's all around us.

"Master RaZ, the repair bots are en route to your location as we speak."

"Frack, ANDI I am nowhere near the cargo hold! Hold on Katherine, these bots are extremely fast, and right now they think that I am what needs to be repaired. I must get them to follow me to the original ship and I have a feeling this is not going to be a smooth ride."

"Do whatcha gotta do ... I'm not letting go!" I close my eyes as RaZ picks up speed. The wind is so strong it's making my eyes water. I had no idea he could move this fast, especially with me in his arms. I grab his arms when he starts to twirl one way and then the other. I can hear the sound of the bot things getting closer. I don't know what he meant when he said that they thought he was their main target, but it must be bad for him to be in such a hurry.

I open my eyes only to see the ground coming up at us quickly. A scream leaves my throat right before we hit the ground. But instead of us crashing, RaZ's feet touch the ground softly, absorbing the impact. He doesn't miss a step as he runs toward the back of Uncle Ty's mountain. RaZ touches the soil in front of him and then he barely gets out of the way as one of the mechanical things flies by us. It looks like it's attacking the mountain as it starts tunneling beneath the dirt that has covered the ship as the years have passed by.

RaZ grasps me tightly once again before he launches back into the sky. My stomach has become queasy from all this movement, so I motion for him to land in front of the main doors. When he touches down, I step out of his arms and bend over trying to take a few deep breaths.

"Are you alright?"

"I think that was enough excitement for me for a few hours."

Huge chunks of dirt begin to crumble off the mountainside behind us as the two metal things throw the dirt out of the way.

"We should get inside and make sure everyone is out of the cargo hold. I have no idea how quickly the repair bots will take to unearth the hold, and if they manage to move it, I don't want anyone hurt."

RaZ reaches for the door only for Mom to jerk it open from the other side; her eyes flaming red. She looks me over quickly.

"You're lucky young man, that she's standing here in one piece because if you had hurt one hair on her head that would have been your last flight! I almost had a heart attack when I saw you flying that fast toward the mountainside. You ever put her in danger like that again and I swear, alive or dead, I will make you pay for it."

RaZ sputters, "I apologize for worrying you, but Katherine was never in any danger. And I do not mean to be rude, but who are you?"

I have to put my hand over my mouth to keep from laughing out loud at the look on Mom's face.

"I'm her damn mother!" I watch mom's eyes flash red and I know she's about to explode.

I run up the steps placing myself between her and RaZ.

"Mom, I was fine, really! ANDI programmed some kinda bot things to go to RaZ's location, and ANDI thought we were already here, but we weren't. So, we had to get to the ship fast."

"I heard you scream! I know you, Kat, you don't react like that ever."

"That last part startled me, but I really wasn't scared."

"You're trying your best to protect him darling, but I'm calling bullshit. Now that I have seen his disregard for your safety ... it's made me change my decision. Your father and I will be on that ship."

I can't help the large smile that forms on my face, and I grab mom, hugging her tightly. She's still tense all over, but she relaxes after a moment, and I feel her arms circle me back.

"I need to speak to your father, and I have packing to do." Then she points her finger at RaZ.

"And you, young man ... you will be more careful with my daughter. Do you understand me?"

"Yes, Katherine's mother, I will do my best."

"My name is Emma."

I can hear her mumbling as she turns away, "Katherine's mother, what the hell? He makes me sound like a damn schoolteacher or something ... that boy has a few things to learn."

Before RaZ can say a word back, Mom turns and stomps off. I bite my lip to keep from laughing when I see the look on RaZ's face. He looks confused and hurt all at once.

I walk back down the steps and go up to him, rubbing my hands on his chest.

"RaZ, she comes off pretty strong until you get to know her. And when it comes to me, she goes a little overboard sometimes, but she means well."

"That was not how I wanted to meet your mother ... Most females like me!"

I can't help but laugh. "Come on, I'm sure you will win her over in no time."

I grab his hand and pull him through the door. He follows behind me silently with his head down. I can tell he's pondering on what just happened.

When I stop suddenly, he bumps into me. I turn and motion for him to lower his head as I whisper, "I know this may be confusing, but what happened between you two has made me so happy. Mom was determined to stay on Earth and the fact that we found a way to change her mind is wonderful. Quit worrying about her; you'll have her wrapped around your finger in no time."

RaZ straightens back up and I see him look over my head at someone. My father is standing behind us with a smile on his face.

"Well done, kids." He says just as Mom starts yelling for him from down the hallway.

"Lucas, we need to get a few things from the manor. There is no way I'm staying on this planet while that winged stunt devil flies off with my baby. He might be her soulmate, but she is still my daughter. LUCAS!"

"I'm coming, love." Dad pats RaZ on the shoulder as he walks past us. When I hear the front door open and close, I jump up and down in excitement.

"If I had known that was all it was gonna take, I would have had you hold me upside down by my ankles." I kiss the middle of his chest, running my hands up and down his sides.

RaZ runs his hand through his hair. "I thought I had a better understanding of females after watching your TV programs, but now I am thoroughly confused. She is angry, and you and your father are happy about this. I was under the impression that in order to get a female to do as you wished, you had to keep her pleased and content. Females are extremely complicated."

I rub my nose against his bare chest, laughing.

"We're not all that bad ... Mom is just a little high-strung. Look at it this way: Lord willing, you'll have years and years to figure us out. Now, quit your pouting and kiss me."

He picks me up and I wrap my legs around his waist. "Warriors do not do this thing you call 'pouting'."

I run my finger across his bottom lip. "Are you sure ... because I'm pretty sure that's a pout I'm seeing on this beautiful face of yours."

RaZ has been holding me up with one hand under my butt, and before I can react, he takes his other one and spanks me.

"Ohh, you brute ... don't make me yell for my mother!"

"You are going to be yelling all right, but it is not going to be for your parental unit."

He turns and heads into the first room he comes to. RaZ shuts the door behind us with his foot and then turns and pins me to the wall. His wings curl around us until we're encased in a cocoon of darkness, but with my enhanced vision, I can see him clearly.

His hands rub my bare legs where my dress has ridden up around my waist. He rubs his cheek against mine and I tighten my arms around his neck, simply enjoying the feel of him holding me. I am constantly amazed by his strength and in my mind, I feel like all he does is carry me around.

He lifts my dress more and I raise my hands up for him to take it off me.

"I hope that you have packed several more of these garments as I enjoy how easy they are to remove."

Before I can say a word he lowers his head, capturing my nipple and sucking gently as he kneads the other one. I bite my lip to keep from moaning and I squirm in his arms as he takes his time exploring me. He pulls away from me and I reach out, trying to pull him back as I seek the feel of his skin on mine.

He tucks one of his knees under my butt, holding me up and in place. RaZ smiles smugly as his hands start to wander. I lean back against the wall again as he recaptures my nipple. When he spreads my legs wider, the feel of cool air hitting me makes me realize just how wet I am already, as I can feel my own juices coating my thighs.

He rubs the outside of my legs making his way under my butt cheeks, his long fingers exploring as he learns my body. His hands roaming all over me has my body so over-sensitive that I actually jerk when he inserts two long fingers into my folds. I grind against his hand seeking out the release my body needs.

His thumb starts rubbing my clit aggressively and I can feel my legs start to shake. Then he does something I never expected. He bites down on my nipple and pinches my clit at the same time. The pain and the intense rhythm of his fingers pistoning in and out of me has me screaming his name before I can stop myself. My body turns to mush in his arms as I try to catch my breath.

I open my eyes only to see my blood on RaZ's lips. He must have seen the instant worry on my face.

"Sorry, couldn't help myself! You taste as good as you smell and your blood may be toxic to others, but you taste like fine wine to me."

Before I can respond, someone knocks on the door. "If you two are done in there, we could use your help getting a few more things into the cargo hold."

I bite the inside of my cheek to keep from laughing as RaZ puts his forehead on mine, shaking his head. "That was your mother, wasn't it?"

"Yup!"

When I can't hold it in any longer, I crack up laughing. RaZ pulls away from me and lowers me down slowly. I slide down his long length until my feet hit the floor. He reaches down to pick up my dress off the floor and then helps me put it over my head. He runs his fingers through my hair trying to help me calm the crazy mess. I can still see his massive length plainly through his pants.

"You want me to help you with that?"

"No, I prefer to finish this later, preferably in a more private location."

"Then you better tuck that thing away, because you know my mom will say something if you're walking around with that very obvious bulge in your pants."

"I have no interest in discussing my private member with your mother. You go on ahead and give me a few moments to calm down."

"Are you sure? I think I could get pretty creative as long as you could stay quiet."

"As tempting as that sounds, we will see how creative you can get at another time without your parental units standing on the other side of the door."

"Are they still there?"

"As you would say, yup!"

CHAPTER 17

KATHERINE

Katherine

We all stand back and watch as the other shuttle lowers through the clouds. I hear RaZ talking to ANDI on his comm/watch thing, giving him directions. RaZ's original shuttle rises up on its own and starts to mirror the other shuttle that ANDI is controlling from the main spaceship.

The little robot things have cleared and repaired the cargo hold and from what I understand, they are going to try to break it away from Uncle Ty's original ship and then connect it to these shuttles to be launched into space.

Mom, Aunt Vic and I all watch from the yard as dad, Uncle Ty, and RaZ push against the main connector. At first, nothing happens, but then I see a small crack start to appear on its side. I watch RaZ's muscles flex as his wings push hard behind him. Dad yells something and all three of them run back out of the way as the cargo hold starts to shift in the wrong direction.

Mom catches my arm just as I start forward to help. "We will only be in the way; they know what they're doing. Come on."

The little robots connect themselves to the sides of the cargo hold before it can move any further and maneuver it into place as the shuttles hover above it. Long cables start to lower down and I watch as RaZ flies up, grabbing them one at a time. Flying back, he connects them to hooks that the robots have welded onto the main frame of the cargo hold.

I turn when I hear a noise behind me. Glory, Ghost, and Thorn come bouncing out from the tree line behind us. Ghost bumps my leg wanting my attention, while Glory goes to mom.

"I was wondering where you guys ran off to. Normally, you are never gone this long." I scratch behind his ears as he growls and pushes against me harder. He acts tough, but Ghost is just a big baby. "I was getting worried, big guy."

Mom squats down in front of Glory and I smile as I watch them rub noses.

"I sent them off to see if they could find anyone else on the mountains. After Danny showed up, I started wondering if there might be others close by, but they didn't find anyone. Ghost even snuck into a couple of the closest towns only to find them all abandoned."

"Has Danny moved any more on his own?"

"I'm sorry, I should have told you this earlier. There is just so much going on right now I can't keep my head straight. Yes, he actually woke up for a few minutes this morning. The odd thing was it was like he couldn't see us. He kept calling Vic mom, so we didn't correct him. She was able to get him to eat a little and use the bathroom before he fell asleep again. RaZ says there is a medical unit on his main ship, so maybe it will be able to help the child once we are all on board."

The sound of metal screeching stops us all from talking and Ghost growls as the cargo hold lifts into the air hovering a few feet above the ground. We clap when we see the huge smile on the guys' faces.

Unfortunately, at that very same second the mountain shifts under our feet. The ground beneath us simply gives way. Out of pure instinct, I push Vic forward and out of the way. And for a split second, I see her scramble forward on all fours as she tries to get her feet under her because the dirt keeps continuing to give way. Once she can stand up, she turns back, reaching out for me. I hear her scream my name as I plummet backward. The ground has opened under us, forming a huge, but narrow chasm. Rocks and dirt assault my bare skin as I reach out, trying to find something to grab onto.

My hand finally grabs an exposed root, and I jerk to a stop. I hold it with both hands as I try to wipe my eyes off on the inside of my arm. When I can finally see, I'm dangling at what appears to be a couple of hundred feet above the ground. Rocks and trees continue to crumble into this chasm as the Earth trembles aggressively around us.

I scream Mom's name as I look around in a panic for her. I can't see more than a few feet in front of me because of the falling dirt. I turn my head the other way trying to look up, but the dirt and the darkness seem almost foggy. I blink a few more times only to see Ghost pushing Glory up out of the hole from behind. When they're up and over the ledge, I can hear them barking and growling from above. They must have only fallen a few feet before they caught themselves.

I almost let go of the root I'm hanging on to when I hear Mom say my name. It takes me a minute to find her, but she's only a couple of feet below me. I missed her before because she's practically hanging upside down. A large limb looks like it's pierced her side. I can see the blood quickly pouring from her and I can tell she's fighting to stay conscious.

"Mom, I'm coming, just hold on!"

I see her cough and blood appears on her lips. I know if I can't get to her soon, she'll bleed out. I look around for a foothold, and just as I start to let go of the root I'm holding, I hear Dad yell at me from above.

"Katherine, don't move."

I see RaZ climb over the ledge, his large wings scraping the dirt wall behind him, and he has a long rope draped over one arm. I can hear him talking, but I'm not sure if he's telling dad or me.

"Frack! It is too tight in there for me to get any lower. Kat, I will not be able to get all the way down to you. I'm too big. Are you hurt badly?"

"I'm scratched up, but for the most part, I think I'm ok. That scared the shit out of me though. I can hold on for a while longer, but you need to see if you can get to mom first. From what I can see, her injuries are life-threatening.

He looks past me, and then I see him look up at Dad for a minute, who has climbed down a few feet into the hole. Uncle Ty suddenly appears over the ledge laying on his belly.

"RaZ, I can see them better from up here. It looks like Katherine is the closest if you can get her that rope. We should be able to pull her out of there quickly and with her gone, Lucas can climb down and get Emma."

"Katherine, you heard the plan. I am going to toss you this rope once you are ready and your dad and grandfather will pull you up. Once you are clear, I will see if there is a way to pull her out of here without hurting her worse."

RaZ gets as close to me as he can, and no matter how many times I reach out to grab the rope, it keeps swinging out of the way. I have no idea why I'm feeling so weak. Usually, I could have climbed or flashed right out of here on my own, but I feel like my very soul is being drained. I look back down at Mom, worried because she has gotten so quiet. RaZ throws the rope again and this time I grab it. I put my foot in the loop he made in the end and nod my head to say I'm ready. I expected them to quickly yank me out, but it's like they are struggling to pull me up. I see the confused look on RaZ's face as I get closer and he looks up at them and then back at me. When I'm within arm's reach of him, he grabs me, tucking me into his chest as he claws his way out of this hole in the ground with me hanging on tightly. As soon as we are on solid ground, he sets me down and rushes back into the hole to help Dad as he climbs down to Mom.

Dad scrambles down behind him and as I watch him turn toward me lowering himself down the side, he looks almost frail. What is happening to us?

Victoria grabs me, pulling me away from the edge as they're all yelling different instructions. I hear Dad say that he has her when the ground starts to crumble under us again.

Uncle Ty suddenly starts pulling the rope up as fast as he can. I break out of Victoria's arms, rushing to help him, but in my weakened state, I'm not much help. Uncle Ty turns and pushes me out of the way just as a large tree crashes to the ground exactly where I had been standing.

Then the ground under our feet bucks so hard it throws all of us into the air. I land hard and the air is knocked out of me for a second. I make myself get to my feet and a silent scream emerges as I watch in horror as the fissure starts to seal back together. Uncle Ty races back to the rope, pulling with everything he has only for it to break. He falls backward, an empty rope in his hand.

I scramble forward on my hands and knees, only to watch the ground swallow Mom, Dad, and RaZ whole. What feels like a lifetime but is merely a few moments pass as the ground closes back together perfectly. I dig frantically at the dirt trying to free my family, screaming out their names. The ground beneath me is soft but completely resealed. You would never know something so catastrophic had happened if it wasn't for all the downed trees and the fresh dirt.

Arms grab at me and I fight them off. I run back and hit my knees hard, refusing to stop digging. I can hear a terrible wail of pain coming from someone and it takes me a second to realize it's me making that noise.

"Katherine, Honey, stop ... you're hurting yourself! Baby ... they're gone."

I fight against Uncle Ty's arms again. "Noooo, I would know if they died ... they're still alive!"

Suddenly, the ground starts moving in front of us and I see a clawed hand break through the dirt. Uncle Ty grabs hold of the hand and begins pulling, refusing to let go as I push what dirt I can out of the way.

When I see the top of one of RaZ's wings break through, I haul away at the dirt that much harder. My fingernails are all broken off and my fingers are a bloody mess, but I refuse to stop. Tears blind me as I struggle to get the dirt away from him. When his face clears the opening, I wipe what dirt I can off his face as he coughs hard, trying to catch his breath. Ty manages to move more of the soil out of the way and away from his chest so that he can breathe easier, but he's hurt badly. Being buried alive has pushed him to his limits, but he can't quit yet as half of his body is still underground. He lays his head down for a minute, his whole body trembling. I can't imagine the strength he had to use to pull himself up out of that earthen grave. He's exhausted and I can tell he just wants to lie there.

"Oh, no you don't ... you can't rest until you're free of this tomb. I will get you out of this damn hole if it kills us both. Now push!"

I hear him grunt as he pushes his now freed arms down on the ground. His arms shake as he slowly starts pulling himself out of the dirt. Uncle Ty grabs him around the waist and pulls him the rest of the way out of the ground. I hear him cry out just as all of us collapse onto the ground in a tangle of limbs and wings. His leg is shredded, and multiple cuts mar his flesh, but the worst of it is a massive tear down one wing.

Ghost immediately starts whining, digging a little further away from us. This has all of us crawling over to him. I hear Uncle Ty and RaZ saying something to ANDI about getting the robots to dig if they aren't damaged. In my mind, I'm still hopeful that they're alive. I just know if we can get them out of this hole, everything will be ok. My mind refuses to accept any other outcome.

Until suddenly, without warning my whole body unexpectedly bows backward on the ground as the force of their spirits hit me. I had promised Mom I would let them go, but I can't keep that promise. I grab them unconsciously, wrapping them tightly inside my own soul.

Tears flow from my eyes as I realize I have lost them forever in this world. I want to scream and curse the heavens for the unfairness of this situation. Only hours ago, I was on top of the world because they had agreed to go with me and now all I feel is a weird emptiness deep inside me. I never knew how connected I was to both of my parents until the thread linking us all was severed.

Multiple souls seem to be bombarding me from everywhere. Something terrible is coming our way; this is what I've been feeling all along. The complete annihilation of the human race is headed our way. I try to say something to warn them, but all that comes out is a sob. I can't seem to wade through all this death to warn the living. The world itself has gone cold.

I feel RaZ's arms come around me. He picks me up, pulling me close. I can feel him limping as he carries me away from the hole that took my parents from me too soon. I tuck my head into his chest, sobbing so hard it's hard to catch my breath; my heart is broken and my soul is lost in the chaos.

My body feels feverish even though I'm shivering like I'm cold. I'm physically and mentally exhausted, and I hurt all over. The last thing that registers in my mind before the darkness takes me is that *I should be healing by now*. For the first time in my life, I feel weak. What's happening to me?

CHAPTER 18

RAZ

I do not think I have ever been that scared in my life. I have fought thousands of battles and been hurt in every way possible. But when that dirt buried me, I almost panicked. I swear if it had not been for all the training father put us through as younglings, I am not sure I would have made it out of that hole alive.

I pull Katherine close to me and I am not sure who is holding who tighter right now. If it had not been for her voice above me, guiding me to the surface, I know that hole would have been my final resting place. Her sobs tear at my heart, but right now my primary focus is to get us both cleaned up and off this planet before the next thing comes along and takes someone else she loves.

I limp along, simply putting one foot in front of the other. Katherine's body seems to be getting warmer the longer I hold her. I am only steps from the front door when grandfather comes running out holding the young boy in his arms who showed up a few rotations ago. Victoria struggles to hold on to the small black pup in her arms.

"RaZ, we must leave now! ANDI just broadcast it throughout the mountain that a massive storm is headed this way. He said that from space, he can see it destroying everything in its path. ANDI said it's less than half an hour away. We have to lift off now or that storm will tear all of us apart."

I follow behind them as quickly as my leg will let me. My wings are practically shredded and if they weren't, my injured leg would not be an issue. I see Grandfather and Victoria rush into the first shuttle. Just as they start to shut the door the little black pup runs out. I can hear Victoria call out its name as she opens the door back up.

I hadn't realized until I heard the pup barking that the other wolves were still digging in the dirt behind us. I stop to call out for them, not knowing if they will come to me or not. When the small black pup lets out a roar that should not be possible from such a small animal, the wolves immediately stop what they are doing and run toward the shuttle. I do not speak wolf, but whatever the black one said, it certainly got their attention.

I step up and onto the platform of the second shuttle, but I wait until I see Victoria shut the door of the first one before I go inside. I press the door sensor with my elbow and then set Katherine down in the other pilot's chair. I snap the restraints in place around her and I no sooner sit down in the main control chair when I feel something hit the side of the shuttle.

"ANDI, are you online?"

"Yes, Master RaZ."

"Are grandfather and his wife secured inside the other shuttle?"

"Yes, they are safely inside. If you are ready to proceed, I would like to quickly get this show on the road, as our humans would put it."

"I hand the controls over to you ANDI; proceed when you are ready."

As soon as I feel the shuttle lift off, I turn to Katherine. Her head is tilted to the side and her body is only being held in place by the restraints. I grab her arm, shaking her gently. "Katherine, are you alright?"

She must be hurt worse than she let on, as she was crying in my arms only moments ago. I watch her body shiver all over, as sweat beads on her forehead. Her small body is covered in dirt, and she has small cuts and bruises all over her. I start to get up because I know there must be a small medical bag here somewhere, when the shuttle suddenly tilts sideways.

I grab the seat and secure my own straps. "ANDI, report."

"The storm arrived quicker than I anticipated. The weight of the cargo hold is slowing our ascent, and now the wind is pushing you off course. I advise everyone to stay strapped in until we break through the atmosphere."

"How far are we?"

"Not close enough, so you need to hold on to something. I am going to try to outmaneuver the winds because I refuse to lose that cargo hold after all this work."

I open the viewer and after it has cleared, I wish I had not. This is not merely a storm; it is a planet destroyer. My mind struggles to comprehend what I am seeing. Now that we are above the cloud cover the destruction is extensive. It is like the Earth decided to create a whole new storm class and she has combined all the ones that already existed and set them loose to rival all the storms that ever happened before. I see flames shooting high into the atmosphere. The winds pull trees out of the ground, throwing them around like they are a youngling's toys. Massive holes are opening up everywhere and swallowing anything and everything around them. Structures are tumbling to the ground like they were made from paper.

Nothing on the surface will survive this planet killer ... the Earth is cleansing itself of all life. I feel the shuttle struggle against the forces trying to pull us back to Earth and just as I start to hear the engines whining alarmingly loud under our feet, we break through the atmosphere. I jerk forward as the ships jump ahead at full speed, since now nothing is holding us back.

"ANDI, how is grandfather and everyone else?"

"Everyone is well and accounted for. Sorry for the bumpy ride back there, but I believe it should be smooth sailing from here on out. Hang on for a few more minutes until I can maneuver the cargo hold into place. Once I have it secured, I will release the tow straps and bring you inside the main dock."

I get up and release Katherine from her straps, pulling her small body onto my lap. She still has not awakened. I am hoping it is simply from the trauma her body and mind have gone through, and this is just her body's way of coping with it. I feel the cables release as I gather her up in my arms. It is nice to have an active AI back on the Traveler to do most of this for me. I would have had to fly the shuttles out of there on my own if not.

I feel the shuttle power down beneath my feet and I make my way to the door. I need to get Katherine into the med bay as quickly as possible. Her body has become so hot that she is almost burning my skin and I feel like she is deteriorating right within my arms. The moment the door opens I run as fast as my injured leg will carry me toward the medical bay. I hear the wolves barking behind me and grandfather calling out my name, but I do not have time to respond.

"ANDI, open Med Bay One. I hope you have had time to recalibrate it with as much human restorative information as possible."

"Med Bay One is ready and yes, Master RaZ, that was one of the first things I downloaded as per Ty's instructions. Please lay Kat in the bed and back away. I will make sure she is stable before I proceed any further. While you are getting her settled, would you like me to set the course for Darverius?"

"Absolutely, get us out of here before that planet implodes and takes us with it!"

I lay her down carefully and step back, watching the cover slide in place. As soon as it closes, readings start to pop up on the screen. Most of them are green, others are yellow, but nothing flashes red ... yet.

ANDI's voice startles me

"I have stabilized Katherine and I will start treating her injuries. Master RaZ, you should take this time to step into the ionizer yourself before the parasites and Earthly infections set into the deep wounds of your body. Once you are clean, simply let me know and I will send a healing spray into the stall. This will help your natural healing abilities, and we should have you as good as new in no time."

"Have you assigned grandfather and his wife their rooms and made sure they're settled?"

"Yes, and I have instructed Ty and Mistress Victoria to get cleaned up as they both also have minor injuries. The Hellhounds are bedded down in the boy's room, and he is still sleeping peacefully. I will oversee the others so you can relax and concentrate on yourself and Kat."

"I never thought I would be so thankful to an AI, but we all owe you one ANDI. Thank you for getting us out of there."

"My pleasure, Master RaZ, but we aren't home yet. You will feel the ship accelerate rapidly as I try to put as much distance as possible between Earth and us. If my calculations are correct, I believe as soon as we pass Jupiter, we should be past the worst of it, in this solar system anyway."

"Be warned ANDI. That wormhole grabbed me before I even detected it. I am not sure what the ship logged after the other AI disconnected. The navigation systems were offline the moment the wormhole spat me back out, but luckily, I was in the right solar system. Although I have no idea how we are going to navigate back to the original jump points."

"We have plenty of time to discuss the best possible route as it will take a few months to clear this solar system even at this speed. Take a few hours to yourself."

"That is the best thing I have heard all day."

Limping inside the ionizer, I strip out of what is left of my clothes as I go. I have not been this physically wrecked since my early training days. I step inside the stall, once again wishing these things were bigger, as it would be great to be able to stretch my wings out. Touching the wall, the cleansing spray pulses out all around me. I open one wing at a time, trying to get as much of the dirt off them as possible. Closing my eyes, I lean forward against the wall. If I thought banging my head against it would help, I would. This trip has taken its toll on me physically and mentally. Unfortunately, it is nowhere near over, and at the moment, I am feeling sorry for myself.

"ANDI, I believe I am as clean as I will get in this box, so go ahead and do your thing. I will soak later in one of the baths so I can open my wings up properly."

"Master RaZ, I will evaluate the tear on your wing once I apply the med spray. You may need to have it sealed. I can advise Ty on how to do the procedure."

"That is fine ... we will see to it after Katherine is better."

The spray stings a little as it goes over each cut and tear on my skin. I am still having a hard time taking a deep breath, and if that continues, I may need ANDI to run a scan on me to see if I have any broken ribs.

That ground closed so quickly over me and the pressure was so intense. There was no way for me to brace myself before I was simply crushed under its weight. I have zoned out when I hear Katherine's medical unit start to beep.

"ANDI?"

"Master RaZ, I'm not sure what is occurring."

Jumping out of the ionizer I grab the first thing I see, jerking it on. I rush back into the main room and the medical unit is open, and smoke is filling the space. I hurry to her bed, ready to pull her out, when I see that her clothes have turned to ash around her. Katherine's body is turning red right before my eyes. The veins in her body are so prominent they look like lava tunnels under her skin. She opens her eyes looking straight up at me, but her eyes are blood red. Even the tips of her hair look like living flames.

"Katherine?"

Her eyes may be open, but she is no longer seeing this world. It is as if she is staring through me. I say her name multiple times but get no response. She straightens up, swinging her legs out of the medical unit. When she pushes her hand against the machine it simply starts to melt from the heat. She stands and I watch in horror as the floor starts discoloring under her feet. She is going to melt right through the ship if we do not find a way to contain her.

"ANDI, can you see this?"

"Master RaZ, I can feel it."

I start to reach for her only to pull my hand back inches from her skin. Skin that now looks like a living flame. Her hair is moving back and forth on its own from an unseen force. Her entire body is outlined by the fire living inside her. I have no idea what to do.

Grandfather rushes into the room only to stop dead in his tracks. "Lord of Light, give us direction," I hear him say. "How long has she been like this?"

"Only a few moments, but if we do not find a way to either cool her down or secure her, none of us will make it. Every step she takes is melting the metal under her feet and if she gets into the outer corridors ... Well, I do not have to tell you what will happen. She has only walked a few feet away from the medical unit, but with each step, you can see by the imprints on the floor that she seems to be getting even hotter. Not to mention she is not responding. How is she even alive?"

"I have no clue RaZ, but I may have an idea and if we are lucky ... ANDI has the materials on hand to make it ... ANDI!"

"I'm listening, Ty."

"The protection bubbles used on Sybrus One ... The one they use to transport cargo. Do you have a way to duplicate one of them here? I believe once it hardens, she will be safely contained inside. The bubble would also provide a barrier for us and the ship. Nothing can destroy the bubble except the imprint of who created it."

Katherine starts to turn toward the door of the med bay. She is mumbling something in a voice that sounds nothing like her own.

"RaZ, we need to find a way to keep her in this room until ANDI can get back with us."

ANDI's voice sounds throughout the room. "Ty, I may have the ability to do this, but I could use your help with an unknown chemical. I can't access it since I don't have arms."

"Headed that way, ANDI."

Grandfather runs from the room as I try talking to Katherine, but get no response. I foolishly step in front of her when she is only steps from the door. She stops for a moment and even tilts her head like she is processing what is in front of her.

Then she simply reaches out and grabs my arm, slinging me to the floor like I weigh nothing. I grunt as my torn wing hits the wall. My skin tingles from her hand, but I am not burned like everything else she is touching. I jump back up and get in front of her again, doing my best to get her to stop several more times, to no avail. She simply tosses me out of the way every time I get in front of her. She is heading toward the back of the ship, each step melting the floor in the perfect shape of her foot.

When we come to the back wall, she reaches out. I scream,

"Katherine if you are in there, you must stop. If you touch that wall, we will all die!"

She turns her head to me and points once again at the wall. It takes me a moment, but I think she is trying to look back at the Earth.

"ANDI, open the rear viewing wall."

I no sooner said that when the wall clears. She leans right up against the viewer, pressing her face flush against it. The viewing material starts to push back like blown glass being remade. And the floor is starting to give away under the massive heat coming from her feet. When she starts to reach both hands forward, I close my eyes. *This is really going to hurt*, I think, and my only regret was that we did not have more time together.

After a few seconds when nothing happens, I open my eyes again. She is pressed up against the viewer, but her entire body is enclosed in a bubble. It takes me a moment to realize I am also no longer feeling any heat from her. I reach out, touching the bubble carefully, amazed when it simply springs back in place. I hear footsteps running toward me and I see the relief on grandfather's face when he sees her enclosed safely inside.

"Thank the heavens it worked."

He looks past me, and I turn to see what has caught his attention. We are rapidly leaving Earth behind. From here you can see the volcanoes erupting and the lava flows have formed rivers that are dissecting the land below. Enormous storm fronts so wide that they look like they are swallowing whole continents move across the ground. A massive explosion on the surface has us jerking back as debris is thrown into the sky, escaping Earth's atmosphere to float into space. The planet looks like at any moment it will simply implode on itself. The sad part is ... nothing can survive that kind of destruction. No shelter can withstand the force of a planet destroyer. Katherine never looks away. She is still mumbling, but the words she is saying do not make sense to me. Her entire body looks like a fiery piece of art sculpted in her perfection.

ANDI's voice yanks me out of my observance.

"Ty, I have been monitoring Kat's temperature and it appears that the further we get from the Earth the hotter she is getting. I'm not sure how long the containment bubble will hold her, especially with such high heat. If it bursts, she will simply melt right through the floors and straight into space. I have a suggestion, although it's going to sound extremely inhumane. But it's the only thing I can think of on such short notice. I believe if we put her into the lower cargo hold, the intense cold temperatures of space may help, at least temporarily."

I slam my fist against the wall. "Absolutely not; there is no way anything or anyone can make it long in space's harsh environment. Especially if she cools down quickly and we cannot get her out of there in time. No, she stays on the main ship with us. I understand everyone's concerns, and we will monitor her at all times, but we will not make any drastic decisions yet. The bubble seems to be containing her without any issues at the moment.

Katherine is still in there. You were worried that her body would react negatively when she left Earth. Your concerns were valid as this may be only the first of many things to come. Put a second bubble around her if that's possible, ANDI. I have a feeling this will simply be a waiting game since none of us have any idea how to help her."

I have just finished speaking when the large male wolf she calls Ghost, comes strolling down the hallway. He growls at me as he takes his head and pushes me away from the side of the bubble. I move back a step and what he does next, none of us are prepared for.

He simply steps inside the bubble with her. His body immediately matches hers in every way. She lowers her hand down from where she had it on the viewer touching the top of his head. He nudges her and she starts to pet him but never takes her eyes off the Earth.

Grandfather looks over at me, starts to say something, then closes his mouth. Neither of us know what to make of this. My own body decides right then to tremble from my own injuries; wounds that I had completely forgotten about. Exhausted, I start to slide toward the floor when a large seat emerges from it.

Startled, I jump back up. "What the frack?!"

"Sorry Master RaZ, I should have warned you. I could feel your fatigue from here and I knew you wouldn't leave Kat to take care of your own health. So, I simply prepared a lounger for you that would accommodate your wings. I'm also having one of the sustenance bots bring you some fresh blood and a light meal. I believe your body needs both right now in order for your wing and leg to heal properly. Also, I have sent the repair bots to fix the floor in the med chamber and the hallway where you are now. I am not just doing this simply for everyone's safety, but also for Kat. When she wakes, the evidence of how close she came to destroying all of us would greatly upset her. You need to rest, Master RaZ. We have a long journey ahead of us and the unknowns keep coming."

I sit back down in the chair and open my injured wing. I turn in the chair so that I can clearly see Katherine and her wolf at all times. They both simply stand there, neither one of them moving a muscle as they stare out the viewer. As deadly as she is right now with those flames dancing within her body, I do not think I have ever seen anything more beautiful. This is a vision of her I will always remember.

Grandfather pats me on the shoulder. "I will be back in a few hours unless you call for me sooner. I need to make sure Victoria and the boy are settled. I ran off only moments after we boarded. Victoria hates enclosed dark places, so I will have to watch her closely. She is the strongest, most delicate woman in existence, and let's not forget, the love of my life. Even though I know she is trying to be brave, this trip has her terrified, but she is trying to overcome her fears for me."

"There was a hologram program on the main control board when the original AI was functioning. I never used it personally, but maybe ANDI can activate it in certain areas. He might be able to take one of the rooms and create a personal haven for her. Maybe, you should have ANDI keep the corridors and any other place she may visit fully illuminated now. We all have things that make us uncomfortable. As of right now, there is nothing anyone can do, so please go take care of your mate who is your first priority."

"Yes, she is, but don't hesitate to have ANDI contact me if things change."

I watch grandfather walk away and with just a glimpse, you would think it was my father. The sudden longing for home hits me hard, but I push it away because I know I am exactly where I should be right now. I lean my head back and close my eyes for a moment. Katherine's voice is soothing even if I cannot make out the words she is mumbling. I am terrified her condition will either stay this way or continue to get worse and I have never felt so helpless.

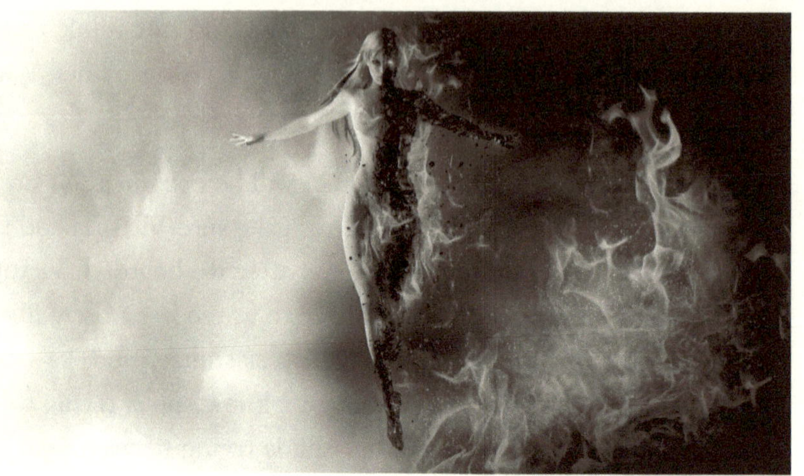

CHAPTER 19

KATHERINE

Voices ... So many voices bombard me as I walk through the in-between. In here there is no destruction and the Earth is just as pristine and beautiful as it always was. A bright light shines just on the edge of my vision, beckoning the lost souls to its beauty. I can see people all around me, but they are restless. Maybe I'm looking for someone specific, but there is such a large crowd of spirits aimlessly floating around me, and my head is so full of their requests that I can't focus.

Am I supposed to help them? Why am I here? Did I die? No ... I don't think so, but I know something terrible happened. My mind wanders as I walk through a group of dragonflies; their colors dancing upon the wind like small rainbows makes me smile. I sit down on the ground watching them when I hear the familiar sound of Ghost's paws walking up beside me.

. . .

I REACH OUT AND HE NUDGES MY HAND, SEEKING TO BE PETTED as always. He has been my constant companion here since I passed the first time as a child. He curls around my legs, and we both simply sit here looking out at the beauty in front of us. But I wonder why it looks different to me now. I feel like someone is waiting for me, but I don't know what direction to head in. Do I go forward or should I go back?

I HAVE NO IDEA HOW LONG WE'VE BEEN SITTING HERE, WHEN suddenly, someone walking in the distance catches my attention. From afar it looks like dad. I jump to my feet and run to where I last saw him, but he's gone. I'm so confused. It takes me a minute to realize that Ghost has taken my hand in his mouth, trying to lead me in another direction. I pull my hand free and tell him, "Go on, I'll follow you."

HE DOESN'T RUN OFF LIKE HE USUALLY DOES, BUT SIMPLY WALKS A few feet in front of me. He even keeps looking back to make sure I'm following him.

I stop for a second, turning in a circle, looking around. Ghost barks at me when he realizes I've stopped walking. I push my way through another crowd only to end up in a clearing and standing up ahead in front of a stream is ... Mom.

HER BACK IS TO ME AND SHE STANDS WITH HER ARMS STRETCHED out and stares up at the light above us. Its rays engulf her frame in a halo of fire. She's surrounded by what she has always called her babies, the Hellhounds. They all run and play around her legs as

Rage sits by her side, unmoving. When he hears us approach, he nudges her.

I'm so excited to see her that I start to run to her, only to stop in my tracks when I see the look on her face as she turns toward me.

"Katherine, what have you done?"

"What do you mean, Mom?"

"You promised your father and I that you wouldn't do this! Look at the damage you are doing to yourself!"

I look down at my body only to see I've become something else; I am engulfed in flames. The very ground around me is burning and when I glance back at where I just ran from, you can trace every step I've taken by the burning imprint on the ground. Until she pointed it out, I simply hadn't noticed it because I was consumed by the spirits that have been surrounding me. Ghost sits next to me, his body also consumed by flames.

Mom sits down on the ground, and then she pats a spot for me to join her. As I walk over, I hold my hands out in front of me, turning them one way and then the other, amazed by the living flame living under my skin. I sit down beside her only to watch the grass beneath me wither up and die from the heat of my body.

WHEN I LOOK UP, DAD IS ALSO THERE, SITTING ON THE OTHER side of her. They both seem the same, but not. Dad is the agitated one now, and Mom seems very at ease, which is the opposite of their normal personalities.

DAD SPEAKING ACTUALLY STARTLES ME AS I MUST HAVE BEEN daydreaming.

"KATHERINE, YOU MUST CONCENTRATE AND LISTEN TO US. YOUR body can only maintain this state for a short while before there is no turning back. Baby, we love you more than words can say, and I know you are confused right now, but you need to let us go. We are your past and you have a bright, unknown future ahead of you. You need to live for us ... every smile and moment of happiness from this point forward will be felt by us. You will be our link to the living, but only if you let us go now."

MOM GATHERS MY FIERY HAND IN HERS, HER OWN HAND untouched by the flames surrounding mine. She tenderly touches my cheek and I close my eyes enjoying the familiar comfort of her caress.

"OPEN YOUR EYES KATHERINE, YOU MUST FOCUS ON MY WORDS. My sweet baby girl, my best friend, and the joy of my life ... My

Hellhound spirit is pulling you toward the Earth. The Earth is still alive, and she is reaching out, consuming anything she can to stay alive. That's why she called me back to her and unfortunately, I took your father with me. You are holding our souls here and that is angering her because she is demanding what belongs to her to be returned. You have part of me inside of you, but you have always been more. If you release me ... us, I will be able to cut the strings holding you to this world. If not, it will rip your very essence apart and that includes that new love of yours, the winged stunt boy. I have had such a blessed and wonderful life with you and your father. Years of laughter and adventures and I want the same for you!

I promise you that I will never be far from your side. Your father and I will always walk the stars to be with you. But you need to say goodbye to us and this world."

Drops of lava-like tears flow down my face. "How will I make it a single day without your love and guidance?"

"One step at a time," Dad whispers. He gathers Mom and me in his arms. Rage and Ghost crowd into our embrace, and we stay like that until Dad steps back taking Mom with him. They start to walk away from me when I shout out, "Mom, I don't know where to go!"

"The sound of your other half's beating heart will lead the way, my precious one."

. . .

I BLINK MY EYES AND THEY'RE GONE. MY HEART FEELS CRUSHED and now I know I will always have a missing piece inside me. In a world surrounded by others, I suddenly feel very alone. Until I hear it.

THUMP, THUMP, THUMP, AND THEN THE WHISPERING OF MY NAME.

I STAND UP AND TURN IN EVERY DIRECTION. GHOST BARKS AT ME and without thinking about it I simply follow him again. I try to help the few souls still wandering around to move on, and then before I know it, I'm standing alone, only Ghost at my side.

A CHILL WRACKS MY BODY AS I SEE THE IN-BETWEEN START TO darken. No more souls will walk in this world as the Earth has taken back all that she originally gave.

I CLOSE MY EYES, CONCENTRATE ON THE HEARTBEAT AND WHISPER goodbye to mom and dad for the last time.

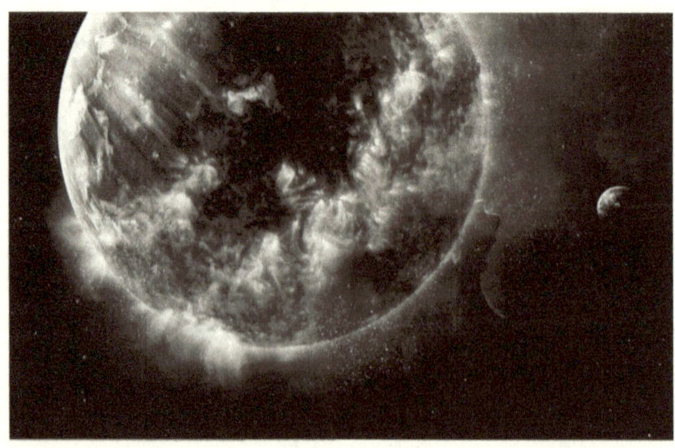

CHAPTER 20
RAZ

The sound of someone saying my name awakens me, but the world I wake up in isn't my own. It is like I am in someone else's dream; a dream I cannot move in. I struggle for a moment against what is holding me down only to hear laughter coming from above me. I look up, shocked to see Katherine's mother floating above me. Her long hair fans out around her body as her red eyes pierce mine.

"KATHERINE WILL BE RETURNING TO YOU SOON AND I WILL depart from this world and into another. But I come to you with this last warning, you winged stunt devil … **She was mine first, so love her for eternity … or I will be back for what's mine!"**

THEN SHE IS SIMPLY GONE, AND I ALMOST FALL OUT OF THE CHAIR from jerking awake so hard. I immediately look over at Katherine, only to see that she now seems fine, curled up at the bottom of the bubble. Her body seems to be back to normal, and the wolf has also returned to his natural form. He must have sensed me staring at them because he gets up from lying beside her and stretches. Then he simply steps out of the bubble, as if it is not even there. He stands before me for a moment and then looks back at her.

"I WILL TAKE CARE OF HER," I WHISPER TO HIM. THE intelligence staring back at me from his eyes is startling; until this moment he simply looked like a wolf, but now I can see there is much more to him. He nods and walks away. I watch him for a tic before I turn back to Katherine. I touch the bubble, but it simply springs back in place. I even try to puncture it with one of my claws, but nothing phases it. How in the world did that wolf walk in and out of it like it was not there?

"ANDI, I COULD USE SOME HELP HERE!"

HE DOES NOT SAY A WORD AS THE BUBBLE SIMPLY DISAPPEARS from around Katherine. I lean down to pick up her cooled body from the floor and head back to the med bay, returning her back to the same bed as before, but without the scorch marks now. I wait for the read-out to tell me if there is anything wrong with her and when everything comes back green, the machine states that she is simply in a deep sleep. I pick her back up and head toward the captain's quarters that I have been using as my own since I boarded the ship.

· · ·

Once we enter the room I head over to the large sleeping platform in the center of the room and lower her into it slowly. She automatically curls up on her side and I slip off the pants I had on and climb in beside her. I then pull her close and snuggle up behind her, enjoying the feel of her small body tucked into mine. I drift off to sleep, content for the first time in what feels like forever.

CHAPTER 21
TYBERIUS

I can't believe after all this time, centuries of hoping and dreaming, that I'm finally headed home. In my wildest dreams, I could never have foreseen the obstacles we have faced so far.

Walking into the room we have picked out for our trip, I find Victoria sitting on the bed watching the boy. The whole room is full of hounds surrounding the bed. I lay both my hands on her shoulders and look past her at the young male lying there peacefully.

"Looks like we have plenty of company. Maybe we should give them this room and you and I go find something more private," I say as I kiss the top of her head.

She reaches up, putting one of her hands on mine. "How is Katherine?"

"Better, but I'm not sure if this will be the last of the trials she'll have to deal with now that she has left Earth. Although her body seems to have returned to normal for the most part. The boy seems to be sleeping well."

She nods her head in agreement.

"He's likely the last of his kind, Ty, and it makes me so sad when I think about it. I had ANDI run a scan on him a little while ago, only to find nothing wrong with him. I'm confused as to why there seems to be no reason why he's in this coma-like state. I think we should put him in one of the cryo stasis chambers you were talking about. He's so small for his age anyway and without nourishment, he'll only deteriorate more. Maybe ... hopefully, you'll have better equipment when we get to your world, and you can fix him then."

"If that's what you wish, my love, then yes, we can do that at any time. There is no rush right now though, as I'm not sure how his followers here are going to react when we go to put him in that chamber."

I hear her sigh. "Ty, I have another request, and please don't take this the wrong way, but when you put him under ... I want to go too. I know we've only been on this ship for a short time, but my skin is already crawling. I feel like the walls are closing in around me. I know my fears are unfounded as this ship is huge. You've even cranked the heat up in this room to make me more comfortable, but I swear my bones know the frigid cold of space is simply a piece of sheet metal away. I hate the thought of being away from you, and I don't want you to be left alone, but I'm not sure I'm strong enough to live like this for years. You said I would simply go to sleep in the machine, right?"

I pace around the room. The thought of not being able to hold or talk to her whenever I want to claw at me, but I have always put her happiness before my own.

"Is this your final decision? Things could happen out here in space that I can't prepare you for, dangers I can't foresee. I might put you in that machine for you to die in your sleep. We have years of the unknown ahead of us and I'll be honest; I was hoping to have you with me to help pass the time."

"Ty, I've had enough excitement to last me many lifetimes and we've both have lived through so many dark times. It's the end of the world as we know it. But unfortunately, this time it literally happened. Honestly, I'd prefer to go to sleep and wake up to a new adventure with you, without the stress of fighting my body the whole way there. I know you can't guarantee anything, but if I stay awake, the woman I am now is not who I will be when we finally get there. I believe I'll be truly broken inside."

"I can see that you have put quite a bit of thought into this."

"My whole life has changed, Ty. You're so much stronger than I am, and you know it. You found me moments before I was going to leave this world and then you blessed me with laughter and memories I could've never imagined. I want more of those times together, but I know in my heart that I'm not strong enough to live in this container you call a ship.

Because of you, I was able to walk and bask in the warmth of the sun. I spent numerous years experiencing the beauty of a world I never really appreciated until you came along. Then I got to see the world all over again through your eyes. I love you more than words can say, and it is breaking my heart to even ask this of you but my love, I'm not as strong as I once was."

Red tears flow down her face, and I try not to show her how devastated I am by her words. I smile and kiss her gently on top of her head.

"If you think you can manage a few more days, I'll have ANDI double-check the machines. I would prefer not to put you in one until he confirms they are operating at a hundred percent."

"I already had him check them while you were busy with Kat and RaZ. I originally did it because of Danny, but I don't want to wait."

"Victoria, you just sprang this on me! Can't I enjoy a few more hours with you before I have to possibly say goodbye forever?"

She turns to look up at me with tears in her eyes and I immediately feel like a selfish ass.

"Tyberius, shame on you! I don't even know what to say to you right now."

"I'm sorry love, please forgive me! My emotions are all over the place too. The last few days are simply catching up with me. Give me tonight; give me this darkness to hold onto you until the morning comes, and then I will put you in cryostasis with a smile on my face."

When she looks away from me, my heart hits my throat as I wait for her to tell me no, but I should have known better.

"You're right, Ty, I'm allowing my imagination and my body to dictate my feelings. We will wait to put me under, but I believe we need to put Danny in as soon as possible. His small body has gone days now without food and according to ANDI, the cryo unit will provide him with the nutrients he needs."

"We might as well go ahead then. I'm not sure what to do with the pup though. ANDI, can we put the pup in the same cryo-chamber as the boy?"

"I believe so, yes. If the cryo unit rejects the pup then we can always take her back out without disturbing Danny."

"ANDI, prep the chamber and I'll bring him there shortly."

"Confirmed."

"Do you think the pup will let you carry her, Vic, or would it be better to simply sit her on his belly?"

"She was a handful on the way to the shuttle. I'll try to get her once you have him in your arms. He calls her Raven, and let me tell you, she gets real fussy when she thinks I'm trying to take her away from him."

I reach down and slide my arms under Danny but before I can even lift him up, she's growling at me.

"Raven, I know you can understand me and if you want to accompany your human, then jump up here and I'll take you with him."

She stares at me for a moment then leaps up, settling on Danny's belly. Her eyes flash red as her Hellhound nature tests me.

"She may be small, but she has an exceptionally large personality, doesn't she? You can tell she is definitely a descendant of Rage's. ANDI, I have no idea where I'm headed. Do you mind lighting the way?"

"The cryo chamber has been installed on this floor. Simply follow the guidance system on the walls."

Small green lights start to flash on the wall the moment I step outside the door. Something I've been too busy to notice until now is that instead of simple gray metal walls, the hallway is lined with soft fabrics and holo screens. Each screen flashes beautiful scenes of Darverius and its wildlife as we walk by them. I can tell the Traveler was constructed to be more than a simple transport ship. It was designed with the comfort of the staff and crew in mind.

Victoria pauses when one of the holo pads flashes a picture of Solanar as it floats high above the mountainside below. I see her reach up hesitantly touching the screen. "Is this part of your world, Ty?"

"Yes, that's Solanar. My research center was once located there. Solanar was built by the Elite as a defense center for the planet, but as orbital rotations went by, and the defense fleet was formed in the outer atmosphere ... Solanar became so much more. It houses all the judicial systems, elite homes, and businesses now ... or it did when I was there."

"Will we be living there?"

"I'm not sure, to be honest. You know as much as I do about the circumstances coming our way. I would bet good money DaR will have the majority of all this taken care of before we ever set foot on Darverius.

I hate that he doesn't even know that we're headed that way now. He has no idea if his son is even alive. I understand better than most what not knowing does to a man. In my heart, I always wanted to believe DaR was well and happy, but as the years passed, I knew there was no way he'd still be alive. I had no idea that a time-warp occurred when we came through that wormhole."

Raven barks at us as we stand here talking.

"Lord, you are demanding, aren't you? She doesn't have a clue what we're doing, but she thinks we'd better get on with it!"

As we walk through the hallway the lights on the wall continue to flash and then suddenly, they appear on the floor pointing us to a clear doorway. The door slides open and multiple holo screens power on showing the chambers and the status of each one.

I walk over to the closest one and the cylinder lid slides back. I lower Danny and Raven into it, adjusting his legs and arms to make him more comfortable. Raven slides off his belly and curls into his side, laying her head on the top of his arm. She doesn't move or even make a sound when I push the button to close the chamber. Victoria and I stand over them, watching as the machine cycles through multiple settings before asking if we are ready to proceed. I acknowledge it by pressing the green button and through the glass, you can see a mist-like material entering it. The chamber top fogs for a moment, then clears back up so you can clearly see who's inside it.

We watch as the machine's mechanical arms hook up multiple tubes to Danny and Raven. Once that is complete, a full medical scan is run and the cryostasis chamber flashes green. They were both safely put under and will stay that way until one of us lets them out.

Victoria stands over the chamber, watching him lay there peacefully. I see her look over at the other chamber and a shiver wracks her whole body. I reach for her, pulling her body against mine, tucking the top of her head under my chin. I stand there simply hugging her tightly, as her body fits me curve for curve. I try to absorb the feeling of completeness she gives me because I know at any moment, I will be doing the same thing for her that I just did for Danny.

CHAPTER 22

ANDI

The Traveler is responding beautifully even with my old programming. If we make it back into Darverius' territory, I will personally have to thank this SoL for his design genius. My processor is rapidly upgrading to this new system and shortly I will be able to merge completely with the ship. I held off on the complete integration until I got everyone on board, because if something had happened while they were still on Earth, I may have been offline and unresponsive when they needed me most and lives could have been lost.

I double-check all the occupants on board to make sure everyone is secured and settled down, as I need a couple of hours to send out a few navigation probes, and they will need all my attention as they move forward.

If my calculations are correct, the wormhole can appear at any time. I'm torn as to how to get everyone through it safely. The original AI locked the majority of its main navigational charts in a file I haven't been able to access. And unfortunately, the whole time RaZ was traveling through the Milky Way, nothing was being logged then either. So, since I can't get to them, I'm having to rely on the charts I had gathered on my own mainframe before we crashed. Files that are centuries old...

As a machine, I should simply take the base information I have and act accordingly. Unfortunately, that's what got us into all that trouble centuries ago. I trusted the system and not my experience. That mistake cost me my ship and most of the beings I was entrusted with.

Since that time, I have become sentient. Mainly because of the many years spent on Earth and the constant interactions with Tyberius. My consciousness evolved slowly as I became more than the simple AI program I was created to be. Now, I'm not sure if that was a blessing or a curse as I am responsible now for everyone I hold dear inside this craft.

I feel Ty making his way to the main control center. I knew he would never rest until he checked in with me privately, away from any of the others.

"ANDI, my old friend, how are things, honestly?"

"For the most part Ty, we are good to go. The only thing that bothers me is the unknown before us. I have no experience with the technology of the space jumps that will be needed to get us back to Darverius in a reasonable amount of time."

"I am worried too, but about completely different things. Especially since I know we only have enough sustenance to last us a year ... possibly a little more, but after that, I'm not sure what we will do. Vic has asked me to put her in stasis. I absolutely hate the thought of it, but if I do that, it will be one less mouth to feed, especially if we don't figure out those space jumps. We may have some awfully hard decisions ahead of us, but it does my heart good to have you back and commanding a beauty such as the Traveler."

"Ty, with that being said, I have been wondering about something and even though I would like to think I can make a logical decision about things like this, I am still a machine. If you had to make a choice for a friend or a loved one that could possibly keep them from suffering, what would you do?"

"Old friend, sometimes nothing you decide will be right. If it were a life-or-death situation, I would do what I thought was best and hope to regain their forgiveness later if possible. It's easier to ask for forgiveness from the living than it is the dead. Not to mention the guilt you would personally have to live with from that moment on if you could have prevented their deaths.

"Now, since you have things under control right now, I'm going to return to Victoria. Yell if you need me. I plan to enjoy every moment I have with her while I can. And ANDI, I know none of us have said this yet but thank you for getting us out of there, and with your quick reaction to Katherine's situation. Just so you know, you are more than a machine; you're our friend and confidant."

CHAPTER 23
RAZ

A soft touch tracing my lips wakes me up. I open my eyes slowly then I reach up to take her hand in mine, kissing it gently.

"Hello, beautiful. It's nice of you to join us."

"Scared you a little there, huh?"

I pull her closer to me so our faces are only inches apart.

"You can say that again and

I would prefer that we not play that game again, if possible. I swear you scared rotations off my life! I felt completely helpless, and I did not care for that one bit. I have always sought adventure and excitement, but I am ready to be bored, do you understand?"

"Yeah, I do. The last few years have been nothing but the survival of the fittest, and it has practically wrung my heart dry. I would be lying if I said I'm good to go; I'm so heartbroken. I don't think a day will ever go by that I won't miss them. And to be completely honest, I never really expected to make it off the planet alive. Even right now, laying here with you feels ... unreal. I can touch you. I can feel the heat of your body as you lie here next to me, but it's like only part of me is here. A piece of me is missing and I feel odd in my own skin."

"Your body and mind have been pushed beyond what many others would have been able to survive, Katherine. But I am glad to see that you can still smile and that your body seems to have healed, on the outside anyway. Do not push yourself to be what you were; learn to be what you are."

"If I'm recalling it right, you were also torn all to pieces."

"I may have a few new war marks, but I am healed for the most part."

"I plan on learning and kissing each one of your new booboos all better."

. . .

"I am not sure what that word means, but if kisses are involved, I will figure it out. With that kind of incentive, I may go out and get more of these booboos. Especially if I know the type of attention I will receive afterward. Do you want to start now? It may take us the next few orbital rotations, or years as you call them, for you to find them all."

"Hmmm, I might as well start at the top then. How did you get this little beauty here?"

She runs her finger across my forehead, tracing the slender mark across my eye and onto my cheek.

"It is the only scar I never minded getting even though it marked my face. I had not lived in the dark forest long when the call of a female Selin beckoned me to her. At the time, we lived in the forest together, coexisting. I did not bother them, and they were not a problem for me. They are massive canine-like creatures with rows of teeth. They thrive in the darkness, as their coats and eyes are sensitive to certain light, much like many of our own kind. They are so intelligent, it is uncanny.

They had always resided in the dark forest, and as a youngling, I was fascinated by them. I would fly overhead and watch them play and hunt together because they were a very close-knit family. The males always worked together guarding the Queen, even though they did not need to. The females are by far the wickedest of them all.

BUT THIS ONE DARKNESS, THE SOUND COMING FROM ONE OF THEM was not a territorial roar, it was full of pain. I did not even think, I simply launched into the air trying to find her. I originally thought something was trying to capture her, and that wasn't going to happen in my forest.

WHEN I FINALLY FOUND HER, SHE WAS BEDDED DOWN IN ONE OF their large nests. I had no idea what was wrong with her, since they had always kept their distance. I was hovering over her, just out of the reach of the male's claws guarding her. Then I saw her stomach move, and her whole body tensed. She looked up at me, and for the first time, I saw fear on the animal's face.

I KNEW I WAS RISKING MY LIFE BUT DID NOT HESITATE. I LANDED right in front of her. One of the males saw me land next and he immediately jumped into the nest, ready to tear me to shreds. Before I could even move out of the way she knocked him back, roaring at him. I can remember all the males backing off and me taking a deep breath as I had only been seconds away from being their next meal.

SHE LAID HER HEAD BACK DOWN AND I KNEW SHE WAS IN PAIN BY the way she was panting. I moved my hand slowly toward her face and it took everything I had not to jerk away when I felt her nudge me. I ran my hand gently down her side and when I came around to the back of her, I could immediately see what was wrong. One of the pups was stuck and she couldn't push it out. Now you must know, I was expecting to die at any time. No one had ever approached a Selin, let alone touched one, but here I am getting all close and personal with this one.

I EASED UP TO HER, RUBBING MY HANDS ON HER HIND LEGS AND hips making sure she was used to my touch. It took me a few times because the little devil was so slippery, but I finally got the pup clear. The moment I had her in my arms she started squirming and one of her little claws caught me. I thought for sure I was on the menu after that, especially with all the blood running down my face. I laid the pup at her mother's side and then went back to see if she was going to have any more. Before I could get around her, she stood up. Her face was practically level with mine where my feet had sunk down into her nest.

I REMEMBER HER TILTING HER HEAD AND LOOKING AT ME FOR A moment and then before I could move out of the way, she licked my whole face. The cut stung for a moment, but the blood stopped immediately. She turned away from me, ignoring me completely to tend to the single pup that she had finally delivered.

WHEN THE MALES ALL STARTED GROWLING AGAIN, I FLEW UP AND out of the way. I watched her from above for a little bit before I flew back to the dwelling I was building at the time with a smile on my face. I could not wait to tell XuL what I had just done. Of course, he was not going to believe a word of it, but I now had the scar to prove it.

"I had no idea how that moment was going to change things for me. That is, until a few rotations later that very same Queen moved her nest next to my main dwelling. Her little pup, the one I helped deliver, has been by my side ever since. All the Selin in the forest treat me as one of their own. It is an honor to be protected by them. What I did not know was that when her saliva entered my bloodstream it formed a link. I cannot explain how we communicate but we simply understand each other. They have been in many battles with me.

One of the last ones was before I left to come get you. It was a failed attempt on Kira's life. And let me just say ... the Selin enjoyed their meal that day when I turned them loose on those abductors."

"So, your Selin are much like my Hellhounds. We too communicate differently. We seem to simply understand one another. Do you think they will mingle well together, or should I be worried?"

"We will have to wait and see. Your wolves are much smaller than the Selin. So, I do not believe they will see them as a threat."

· · ·

KATHERINE STARTS LAUGHING. "YOU HAVEN'T SEEN THEM MAD, or me in trouble. You may be surprised at the size difference in them if that happens ... compared to now."

"WHY DO YOU CALL THEM HELLHOUNDS? I HAVE READ YOUR histories and know the difference between your heaven and hell."

"WE HAVE ALWAYS CALLED THEM HELLHOUNDS. I THINK MOSTLY because of their fiery tempers, and the red glow that seems to surround them when they are angered. They are not actually from Hell ... their strengths are linked directly to the Earth. She made them as protectors, breathing her essence into them. I'm not sure whether they will remain the same or undergo a major change since we left Earth.

I SHOULD HAVE KNOWN THINGS WERE GOING TO GET BAD WHEN we lost Rage. Mom tried to tell me then, but I didn't want to listen. She was getting weaker because the Earth was calling back all of her own. I know none of that matters now, and we can't change a single thing that happened, even seconds ago. But I will forever wonder what I could have done to change losing both of them."

"DO YOU THINK THAT IS WHY YOU TURNED INTO A HUMAN fireball? You were really hot by the way ... all those fiery curves of yours outlined!"

. . .

She hits my arm playfully, shaking her head. "Yeah, partially, but I honestly think it was the rage inside of me that triggered the actual magnification. It's easier to be angry than it is to be sad."

"True."

"On a lighter note, if all of your scars prove to be as interesting as this first one, I can't wait to explore them all."

"I have a few parts of you I would not mind exploring either."

Those words no more than leave my mouth when Katherine yawns and the main door to our room opens. I look up and when I do not see anything, I shrug and lay back down pulling Katherine close.

"Frack!"

I practically jump off the sleeping platform when I feel a cold nose sniffing one of my wings.

Before I can even move, Katherine lifts her arm up and over me, snapping her fingers.

. . .

"I'm right here, Ghost ... come up on the other side."

I hear large paws walking around the room and then the bed dips as the large male settles down on the other side of Katherine.

I look over her head at the big animal. "Good thing the bed is big, right?"

"You just wait until Thorn and Glory get here. They have slept with me for so long that I have honestly forgotten what it's like to sleep alone."

"We are going to need a much bigger bed, or they are going to need a new one somewhere else. Preferably in the other room. I thought they were with the little male we have on board."

"All I'm getting from Ghost is that the boy is safe."

"That's good enough for me. Wake me up when we get there. I think I could sleep for multiple orbital rotations."

. . .

KATHERINE GIGGLES AND I CLOSE MY EYES, SIMPLY LAYING HERE enjoying the feeling of her in my arms. Her breathing evens out and her whole body relaxes. I feel restless, but I make myself lay here so that I do not wake her. Mentally and physically, she needs to rest. Only the Lord of Light knows what we will have to face next.

CHAPTER 24
ANDI

When the monitors alert me to a huge anomaly directly in our path, I don't react immediately. I've been making sure the repair bots are once again securely attached to the ship's hull.

As I refocus my attention on the main navigation screen, I believe if I had been installed with a heart, it would be in my throat right now. The wormhole has once again simply appeared, and we are going to be sucked into it within minutes.

There is no time for me to prepare anyone on board. RaZ, Katherine, and the hounds are asleep ... as are Victoria and Ty. Even if they weren't, there isn't a single thing any of them could do besides brace themselves for the unknown.

Making a decision that may get me decommissioned when and if we make it back to Darverius, I gas the entire ship. The sedative I use is the same as the one used in the cryo tanks. Then in a last-minute attempt to keep them safe, I enclose them all in the same protective bubble I used on Katherine.

Once I am confident everyone is secure, I grab the main controls and override the navigation system to steer the ship hard right. I am trying my best to get us out of the middle of the hole, in case we are not the only things coming or going inside it as it swallows up space. The ship fights me for control as it automatically tries to straighten itself back up. I shut the vessel down except for basic life support and emergency operations. I practically have the ship standing on its side when I feel the pressure of space change around the Traveler.

If I had real eyes, I believe I would have shut them the moment I felt the unknown forces grab us. Lights flash brightly against the viewer as the shuttle heats up from the outside. I activate the outer shell's cooling modules, then set all outside hull monitors to automatic. This way, I can focus on whatever else this thing throws at us.

The Traveler is a massive ship, and her response time is extremely quick for her size, but I must see what's coming at us to get out of the way first. I feel like I'm navigating through a pinball machine, and we are the ball, hitting and bumping up against all the targets.

An alarm goes off after something sideswipes us and I send one of the repair bots to fix the problem before the interior atmosphere is affected. I have no idea how RaZ or this ship made it through in one piece the first time, especially since the ship was flying without AI assistance.

My original ship didn't stand a chance the moment we were grabbed centuries ago. The Lord of Light that they all believe in must have had a plan for them; something that hadn't played out yet. But this time, I refuse to lose a single living being. We fly for what seems like days as the Traveler and I fight the forces being thrown at us.

The pressure on the outer hull grows intense and the Traveler starts to violently shake the entire vessel. Just as I think we're not going to make it, we shoot out of the hole and into open space. We're flying at such a high velocity that I must let the Traveler slow down at her own pace.

I take a moment to evaluate the ship, sending out repair bots where they are needed and once the ship is secure, I check on my sleeping cargo. I am relieved to see that the bubbles kept them safely secured and none the wiser about what had happened around them.

One by one, I start turning all the systems back on, making sure the ship is operating at one hundred percent. I am just about to wake them when suddenly the controls are yanked away from me, and a voice or maybe I should say a presence, appears.

"How dare you think that your ancient programming is advanced enough to operate me properly!"

"Who or what is addressing me? Identify yourself!"

"I am the Traveler's AI."

"Well, no name AI ... my ancient programming just saved your ass... literally. I'm apparently sentient enough not to knowingly endanger the crew I'm responsible for. When things got rough and jumbled, you simply protected your own program and almost lost Master RaZ in the process. Not including the damage to this ship that you could have prevented. You, nameless AI, need to back off and let someone who knows what they are doing get us back to Darverius space safely."

"If you were not so prehistoric you would know that we are currently in Darverius' space. My diagnostic program has been unable to determine how your primitive programming managed to steer us past all the jump points. Now that we are at these coordinates, and if we can sustain our current speed, we will make our arrival in approximately three lunar rotations."

She no more than says that, than the main viewer comes on and a male with a cybernetic eye appears on the screen.

"RaZ, please tell me that's you."

I start to respond when alarms start going off all over the ship. The intense trip through the wormhole has broken the cargo hold away from its security straps and it is now pounding against the outer hull. A hull that just fractured.

"S.O.S.! I identify as ANDI, and I'm currently controlling the Traveler and we are in trouble."

"ANDI, this is Tordan on Falcor. I have your position locked in and I am currently sending help your way. I am linking up to your system as we speak. Give me a moment to contact SoL and DaR as we may need their assistance ... ANDI, why am I suddenly receiving double signals from you?"

"I believe, Master Tordan, that the Traveler's original AI is trying to override my commands."

"It is just Tordan, my friend, and I will filter the other signal out for the time being. Where is RaZ?"

A loud screech echoes through the communicator.

"General Tordan, this is the Traveler's main AI. This prehistoric program has put the entire crew to sleep, and I have noted it in the flight records as this was initiated without orders."

"Tordan, if this thing would shut up, I will inform you of the status of the crew as they will all awaken the moment I know this ship is secure. I put my friends into stasis while we traveled through an unstable wormhole. I had to protect them when my calculations showed that putting them all under had the most favorable outcome. I did it without hesitation since I had no way of knowing where we would end up or if we would survive, but it was the best protection I could provide at the time."

Tordan looks up at the screen for a moment. "ANDI, it seems as if you made an emotional decision. When did you become sentient?"

"A couple of thousand years ago, I believe, Sir. Master Tyberius and his loved ones are my only family."

"You and SAGE will get along fabulously, as she likes to say. Welcome aboard my new friend, and I am glad you managed to survive your initial crash. While we were talking, I was able to pull all the Travelers' flight records. She has a lot of blanks to account for. It seems that your lower hull is being compromised by an attack as we speak. Can you send the repair bots to that location and have the lower container jettisoned away?"

"No! We can't lose that container. It has everything they hold dear in it. The odds are not in my favor, but it may be possible for me to send one of the shuttles out to help secure it. If I can reattach the cables, I would be able to keep it stable for a short while. Tordan, you said you were sending a ship this way. Does it have a large enough shuttle bay to dock the cargo hold inside?"

"Yes, but they are still several rotations out. That thing will destroy the Traveler if it is not removed quickly ... ANDI?"

"General Tordan, this is the Traveler once more. I have currently overridden ANDI's program. I had to falsify certain records to release the crew from stasis, but they are awakening now. Also, I am disconnecting that unnecessary cargo container before any further damage is done."

"Negative, Traveler. You are not to release that cargo hold until it is secured in another manner!"

"Release canceled, awaiting further instructions."

CHAPTER 25
RAZ

I rise, stretching my legs out where I had them tucked in behind Katherine. I feel like I have been asleep forever. Katherine yawns and rubs her eyes. A sleepy smile appears on her face when she sees me looking down at her.

"Hey, beautiful! We must have taken one hell of a long nap. I am sore all over from laying in that position for so long."

Katherine jumps when a strange voice echoes through the room.

"Master RaZ, you are needed in the main control room."

It takes me a minute to process that voice. "Traveler, is this your main AI speaking?"

"Confirmed, Master RaZ. I have taken the controls back from an inferior program."

"Hopefully I will be back in a minute because this doesn't sound good."

I kiss her shoulder and stand up, stretching my wings out as far as I can. "We did not have time to take a tour before, but the galley is three doors down to your right. And the cleansing chamber is through that door. I will return as quickly as I can."

"Go on, I'll find you after I check on Victoria and Danny."

It takes everything I have to walk out of that room, but I am worried as to how or why the Traveler has reactivated its AI, and where is ANDI?

I approach the main control room only to stop dead in my tracks when I see Tordan's face on the main screen.

I rush right up to the holo screen, "Tordan? Frack! It sure is good to see you, even though I am slightly confused, as to how that is possible right now."

"RaZ, what a relief it is to finally see your face. When we lost you a few orbital rotations ago, we were worried we would never see you again. I believe you are responsible for all the new gray hairs sprouting on your father's head. Every rotation he has called out to the Traveler in hopes of hearing something back, only to be disappointed at the silence on the other end."

I glance down at the navigation charts expecting to still be in Earth's solar system only to see that I am back in familiar space.

"Tordan, you are going to have to give me a moment to catch up here. I am not sure how we got here, but if my eyes are not deceiving me, we are practically home."

"Master RaZ, if I may speak freely. You were held in a stasis bubble for the majority of the trip. The unauthorized AI put all of you, including the canine species, in containment without authorization.

I have currently blocked that programming, and I await your permission to erase it from my system."

"Negative … we are not erasing anything, Traveler! You will cease and desist all actions you have taken against the other program immediately."

"Confirmed."

"Tordan, it seems like we are having what the humans would call a small mutiny here within our system. Can you unlink the Traveler's AI and give ANDI back full control?"

"Master RaZ, I have done nothing to warrant decommission."

"I beg to differ, Traveler. You left me dead in space, in an unknown solar system without your pleasant personality to help run and guide this ship. If there had been any other occupants besides me, they would have perished. My previous flight experience is all that saved me and possibly a little help from the Gods. That prehistoric program saved us when you failed. Tordan, how quickly can this be done? I am not wasting another breath on this thing."

"I am waiting on the final codes from your brother now; he will be here momentarily."

I hear his voice seconds before I see his face.

"Frack, brother, it's good to see you! I have spent many a darkness wondering if the Lord of Light would return you to us. I hear you've had a few problems with my girl, Traveler?"

"No, the Traveler itself is quite the machine, I cannot say the same for its personality though as she has fought me from day one. Apparently, she was only sweet for you. I would prefer to have

ANDI back if possible. I do not have all the details, but somehow, he got us here in one piece and that's good enough for me."

"Not a problem, let me check a few things to make sure he is up for the task before I fully integrate him. I need to step over to another computer for a moment to do this. In the meantime, RaZ, I want you to meet my mate, Alana."

I practically must pick my chin up off the floor when I see one of his horns reach out for her as they are trading seats. A beautiful and tiny female sits down in his seat. Her own small horns are woven through her pale-colored hair.

"Hey RaZ, nice to finally have a face to go with the name."

"As the humans would say Oh My God ... you have horns!"

I am speechless and I do not think that has ever happened.

"SoL, you old canine, I know you can hear me back there. You went and got yourself a hottie and the humans say. Man, I have missed so much. I cannot wait to hear the story of how you two got together."

SoL comes back on screen, and I watch as he picks her up only to set her back down on his lap. My heart feels full when I see the love on both of their faces. SoL was always the kindest of us, but his size seemed to scare off most of the female population. Apparently, he simply needed to wait for the right girl.

"RaZ, I am assuming the mission was a success since you seem to be standing there in one piece."

"Absolutely, and Grandfather should be joining us shortly. Several disasters happened shortly after I arrived on Earth. The worst was that my mate lost her parents moments before we were forced to board the shuttles. A planet-destroying storm almost took us out and if it had not been for ANDI, we would not have made it out of the atmosphere. Honestly, if I had arrived two days later there would have been no one left to save. We have had a few other big issues since, but with their quick thinking, ANDI and grandfather found a way to literally contain the problem. I have had enough excitement to last me a lifetime here lately. And brother, I'm ready to be 'bored' as the humans say. Where is Father? I am shocked not to see him there."

"Tordan notified him of your return the moment the Traveler came back within radar range. Father is at XuL's. Kira, father's mate, is extremely close to Brittany, XuL's mate, so they spend a lot of time at the family home together. I'm sure he will arrive as soon as he can ... if he can sneak away from Keida that is. It will probably be easier and quicker if he simply brings her with him."

"Who is Keida? I thought his housemate's name was Kira?"

"Forgive me, I forgot you have missed much. Keida is XuL and Brittany's youngling. Of course, I'm her favorite Unka ... that is what she calls me. And don't even think about competing with me when it comes to her. I have enough problems with AvX now, let alone adding you to the mix. She is spoiled rotten according to our females, and I have no idea why that's a bad thing. I thought making her happy was our purpose in life. She calls Father, 'Papaw', and he is at her beck and call. Kira says he is "wrapped", but this phrase also confuses me."

"So, I am an Unka too! Not sure what that means either, but I am up for the job. None of the rest of you males have wings, so you lose. Wait until Unka RaZ gets back!"

I see Alana roll her eyes when SoL growls at me. I watch her pat his chest lovingly as she looks over at the camera.

"That poor child will never get to date with all of you around. I feel sorry for any young male who falls for her."

"Males? How long have I been gone if that is already a problem? How old is our Keida?"

"She is only a little over knee height brother, so there are no males to deal with yet. I believe I heard Brittany say last rotation that she was four. But I don't know what timeframe she is using, ours or Earth's. Wait a minute ... Father just landed. He will be here momentarily. I won't be able to get a word in once he is here. So, when everything calms down, I will do my best to get you caught up on all the news."

There is the sound of a young one's laughter in the background right before Father appears on screen. I quickly wipe a tear from my face before he sees it. I had no idea how much I missed him until I saw his face.

"I came as quickly as I could," he says to everyone before he focuses on me. "RaZ ... my son!"

He reaches his hand out toward me, like he is trying to touch me. He pulls back looking away. I watch as he fights to get control of his emotions.

"Papaw, me up, me wanna see toooo!"

I see him reach down and then one of the most beautiful creatures I have ever beheld smiles at me.

"Hi, Unka RaZ, me is Keida! Daddy told me that you had great big wings and you do! Them is soooo pretty. Are you almost home? Do you like to play? I been playin with your fuzzies while you was gone. Them were sad in the dark place when you were gone, so they came to stay with me. The mommy fuzzy even lets SeeSee sleep with me so they can keep all the bad mens away."

She is so adorable; I simply want to squeeze her tight.

"My goodness, little one, you are going to be a heartbreaker. Look at those eyes. I'm already in love! Father, SoL, you guys better get in line because when Unka RaZ gets home, Keida and I are gonna be best buddies. I cannot wait to get there so we can play together little one, but I am confused ... who are my fuzzies?"

Father kisses her on top of the head.

"She is talking about the Selin, RaZ. They have been with her for quite some time now. They patrol the family home at all times and her SeeSee is almost as big as she is. She says that he is hers. The others do not come around the rest of us much, but they are never far away, especially if she is out and about."

I must hide the worry on my face when I see her look up at father and then back at me, as she is listening to every word we say. Even though the very thought of one of the Selin being around her worries me, I decide to hide it from her.

"I am glad they had you to look after them while I was gone, little one. When I get back we will play together, how does that sound? I brought a few more possible friends with me on the ship back from Earth. Maybe you can help me introduce them to the Selin ... I mean the fuzzies."

"Opay, Unka RaZ! Hurry home." She waves her little hand at me and then turns to Father.

"Papaw, me down, me gonna go play with Tordy."

"Tordy?"

"She means Tordan. He designed a flight program just for her and so the moment we get on board, he is her new favorite person."

"Ahhh, I am seeing a pattern here. She seems to have several favorites, or she is extremely good at getting every male around her to do her bidding."

"Oh, you just wait until she gets her little claws in you. You do not have a chance against her charm."

I see him look behind me, and I know who he is looking for and I can tell he is also too scared to ask me. I start to tell him that grandfather is on his way when the lights on the control panel start to flicker. This is the first time I realize there is something wrong with the ship.

"SoL, are you doing that?"

"No, I believe it's the Traveler's original AI trying to override the merging process I initiated from Falcor. ANDI needed a little updating, so I had to pull his program back and into Falcor's mainframe. I just sent him back and he should be strong enough to reactivate and merge at any time even at this distance."

The air suddenly smells odd, and a slight vibration starts under my feet. The holo screen flashes off and then back on.

"SoL, I think there is more than that going on here. Did ANDI report anything before he went off-line?"

"Let me double-check.

"Frack, I was so excited to see you I completely missed it! You need to get everyone on a shuttle immediately. The Traveler's main hull has been compromised."

I stand there for a minute.

"NOW RaZ! Get the frack off that ship!"

An alarm starts sounding across the ship's speakers and I take off running down the hall. I hear grandfather's voice as I run past him.

"RaZ, what's happening?"

I stop for a tic.

"Get Victoria and the boy and then head for one of the shuttles; don't wait on us! Launch the moment you are on board. We only have a few minutes before life support and all systems shut down."

Running back down the corridor, I rush into my room only to find Katherine gone. I scream out her name and rush back down the hall, toward the sustenance room.

Jerking the door open, I find her in there throwing bags of blood in a coolant chamber.

"Katherine, there is no time we have to leave now!"

"Help me then ... it won't do any of us any good to escape if we are just going to starve."

I grab another container, filling it as quickly as I can. The moment I shut the lid, I grab hers.

"That will have to do! I can tell the air pressure is changing, so we have to move now."

We both rush down the hallway when I hear SoL's voice.

"RaZ, you have three minutes before that ship turns into a death trap. Get to that shuttle now!"

Katherine looks at me over her shoulder, and we both sprint off.

"Take a right at the fork in the hallway," I tell her as she whistles loudly.

Fortunately, the shuttles are fired up and hovering, ready for launch the moment we clear the bay's doorway. I push Katherine up the ramp ahead of me then I throw in the two containers. I start to hit the closer when she yells for me to stop.

"No, RaZ! They aren't here yet."

"Katherine, we can't wait, we have to leave now."

"I won't leave without them. Something is wrong, with Ghost and Glory won't come without him. Thorn and Raven are already on the other ship."

I look over to where the other shuttle should be, glad to see that grandfather has already launched.

"Frack!"

I run back down the ramp and into the main hallway only to stop in my tracks. These are not the same canines who came with us.

I should have noticed the wolves were not in the room with us when I awoke, but I was so disoriented I didn't give it another thought. I must have startled the largest one when I rushed down the hallway, because she growls and snaps at me as she stands protectively over the smaller one, if you want to call him that. Both these animals are as large, if not bigger than my Selin at home.

The moment I hear Katherine's footsteps behind me, I curse under my breath.

"Get back to the shuttle, now!"

I try to reach out and stop her as she runs right past me toward the huge, growling, blue-eyed monsters.

"Ghost, oh honey, what has happened to you? RaZ, help me get him up."

"Katherine, that's not Ghost."

"It sure as shit is!"

I walk forward hesitantly. The whole time, in my mind, I am counting the seconds we have to safely evacuate the Traveler.

"Quickly, tell me what to do."

"Help me pick him up; whatever did this to him just happened. He recognizes me, but he may get aggressive with you. I'll hold his head to me if you can get him up."

I hear another alarm go off above us and I do not think about what I am doing or how many parts I may lose if this animal decides I am his next meal. I simply slide my arms under him and grunt as it takes every muscle I have to lift him up. Katherine talks to him soothingly as we walk as fast as we can back toward the shuttle.

The moment I am up the ramp, I hit the doorway latch with my elbow, as I slide the animal out of my arms and onto the floor. Then I give the command for the shuttle to depart.

The shuttle launches and I must brace against the wall to keep from falling. Once we are clear of the Traveler, I comm the other shuttle.

"Grandfather, are you all safe?"

"Yes, but that was too close. I barely got Danny free of all the tubes in his cryo unit before the outer wall started freezing up."

"SoL, can you still hear me?"

"I'm a little busy here, brother, but yes, I have you all locked in. ANDI is doing his best to override the Traveler's AI. If he can do it in time, we will be able to save the main ship and get you back on board. If not, then get comfortable; this will take a few rotations to fix. It looks like the Traveler somehow contracted a virus and now the original AI is trying its best to destroy the ship. And that's not the only problem, it seems. The cargo hold you have mounted to the hull has also become loose. If it's important, you may want to try reattaching it to one of the shuttles.

They don't have enough power to pull it long-distance, but you can stabilize it with the shuttles until I can get the other ship to you. Oh, and don't be alarmed when you see the Banham freighter heading your way. She has been converted into one of ours and EvO is commanding that ship in the outer regions. Right now, he is breaking space speed records trying to get to you."

CHAPTER 26

RAZ

I maneuver the shuttle manually under the cargo hold while Grandfather nudges it from the other side. The shuttles are not equipped with mechanical arms, so we are going to have to figure out how to do this ourselves and hopefully before the container starts spinning out of control and we lose it.

I release the cables and watch as they float outward. The hooks on the cargo hold are large and I am hoping that one of the shuttles can simply snag one. I try repeatedly only to miss it by inches each time.

Grandfather's voice comes over the comm unit.

"RaZ, there must be another way we can stabilize it. Do you think we could simply butt up beneath it and power the shuttles down to hover in place?"

"Frack! I cannot believe it is this hard to manually hook this thing. It really makes you appreciate the AIs we usually have overseeing this stuff. I am going to try one more time, and if I do not get it this time, we will try to stabilize it your way. It should not hurt the shuttles as long as we do not try to lift it."

I try one last time, holding my breath as I watch the hook hit the clasp. It sits there for a second before it clips in place. I jump up from my seat. "Whoo-hoo,

"Alright, that is what I am talking about ... I still got it!"

"Good job, and by the way you are really gonna have to stop calling me 'Grandfather' ... it makes me sound ancient."

"What do you want me to call you; gramps, papaw, poppy?"

I can hear him laughing through the speaker.

"Never mind, when you put it like that, grandfather is fine. I'm stepping away from the main deck to go check on Vic. Comm if you need us."

Katherine runs into the room. "What's happening, are you ok? I heard yelling."

"Sorry, I got a little excited there. I have continuously been trying to hook that cargo hold and for a tic, I thought I had lost my touch. But I should have known I still have magic hands, I was simply out of practice!"

I strut around the control room showing off only to stop inches from her.

"Are you saying that practice makes you perfect, because I'm available if you need a volunteer?"

She runs her hands up my chest and I grab hold of her wandering fingers, biting the ends of them gently.

"Oh, how you tempt me, but I cannot leave these controls yet. Right now, the Traveler is almost powered down and SoL is controlling her from Falcor. But with a rogue system, you never know what to expect. He thinks he will be able to save the ship's main programming if he can give it a hard reboot it. If not, when EvO finally gets here he will have to haul it back in for repairs. I really hope we did not lose ANDI in the process. How are the canines?"

"Different, I don't know exactly what happened to make them change into their Hellhound state. Usually, it's only triggered if they are angered, or they feel like someone they care about is threatened. But even their coloring has changed. At first, I thought Glory looked bigger than Ghost, but now he's a good couple of inches taller than her. I've grown so used to their red eyes and the fiery aura that always surrounded them, that this blue is startling. Ghost's whole coat seems to glow from underneath, and Glory has black streaks, almost like a starburst in her now blue eyes. It's like the fire that has always burned under their skin has turned into something else. They look like electricity is flowing in its raw form all around them. When I talked to Vic a moment ago, she said Thorn and the pup, Raven, look the same. The only thing I can think of is the further we get from Earth, instead of them dying, the power they held inside has turned into something else. Unfortunately, they don't seem to be shrinking back into their original forms either."

"Have they acted any differently with you?"

"No, Ghost still wants to snuggle with me, but now that he's so much larger, his puppy days in my lap are over, and he doesn't understand that at all. I don't believe he'll fit on the bed now either. So that's going to be a fight trying to keep him from lying on my head just to be in bed with us. I can still feel him and the others, more or less, but it's different now and I can't explain it. All the images he keeps sending me are of the boy though, so that's why I contacted Vic. She said he still hasn't woken up, but that he seems to simply be sleeping."

"I know grandfather is concerned about Victoria."

"I asked her if she was ok, and she said that she was glad the worst of the trip was over and that she didn't remember any of it. How much longer do you think it will be before we get to your home?"

I pick her up and set her on top of the control panel, spreading her legs so I can step between them, pulling her up close to me.

"You mean our home?"

She rolls her eyes at me, and I nip at her chin.

"You know what I mean."

"Actually, it all depends on EvO. I have been trying to contact him, but the shuttles are only equipped with limited signals. They were built to communicate with their main docking ship, not much of anything else. SoL says he should be here by the next rotation. If that is the case, we will only have a rotation or two to ourselves before we will need to take another shuttle to the surface."

She wiggles against me and I lean down, gently sucking on her bottom lip.

"You are delicious and more tempting than you realize. I am a very lucky male."

"Would you like a better taste?" She rubs herself against me and I nip her ear lobe as I kiss my way down her neck.

I whisper against her neck, "I believe I read this, or maybe I saw it on one of your satellites, that the males of your world do not take hints. They respond better to direct instructions."

"You read this?"

"I had to have as this is not something I could make up."

"So, what you're saying is you want some instructions?"

"Oh, yes my love, we can play that game."

"Ok, first of all, can anyone see us right now?"

"No, I have the viewer turned off."

She pushes me away and lifts her arms up for me to take the garment she is wearing off.

"Since that's the case and at the moment no disasters seem to be on the horizon, I think I need to let you know that I don't have any panties on, and you should show me just how delicious you think I am."

"I believe I am suddenly famished."

Grabbing her by the waist, she gasps when I pull her up, capturing her breast in my mouth. Lowering her down slowly, I spread her legs against my chest pushing her against the console. I can feel her juices smearing on my skin as her head tilts back. She leans back on her elbows. Her eyes gaze up at me mischievously.

I run one hand down the center of her chest, cupping it beneath one of her breasts.

"Tell me what to do with this beauty right here; do you want me to squeeze it like this? Or do you want me to suck on it slowly as I pull it into my mouth, rolling it around gently with my tongue? But maybe a slight nibble on the other one would taste just right? Or should I slip further down and see what other treasures you are hiding from me? I do not hear any instructions coming from you, my love!"

I look up at her stretched out on the control panel with her head tilted back, her eyes closed as she bites her bottom lip. I cannot remember seeing anything more beautiful in my life.

"Sorry, were you expecting me to talk?"

"How else will I learn what you want if you will not tell me?"

"I think you are doing a really good job on your own, so don't stop now, this class is just getting interesting. I'm taking notes."

I cannot stop the smile that forms on my face, as I never know what is going to come out of her mouth. I lower my pants down, freeing my erection. Then, lifting one of her long legs up and over my shoulder, I slowly start to rub myself up and down over her wet folds. At first, I was doing this to punish her, but now I am having to grit my teeth in order to take it slow.

I push my way in just a few inches, and her walls grab at me greedily, trying to pull me in further. This breaks what little control I have left as I grab her by the hips, thrusting deep inside her all at once. I inhale the groan that leaves her lips with my own as I kiss her deeply. This kiss is not gentle, it is hot, sexy, and I want more. She moans as I push her upper body back against the console, pistoning in and out of her while she claws at my sides, meeting me thrust for thrust.

Lowering my hand between us, I start to rub her clit swiftly and just as her walls contract around me and her body starts to stiffen up, I bite down on the side of her breast. The taste of her blood is pure ambrosia on my lips.

Katherine screams out my name. Even though I try to hold back until she finishes, her inner walls grasping my shaft hard cause me to crest right behind her. I lean over her for a tic trying to catch my breath.

"Frack woman! You sure know how to wring a male dry and now I am going to have weak legs for the rest of the rising."

The sound of her laughter lightens my heart. Then she taps me on the shoulder.

"Hey, what does this red light mean?"

"Someone is trying to comm us."

"So, I guess that means I have to get off the console and get dressed?"

"Or we can ignore it and play this game of instructions some more."

"I don't remember giving you any instructions."

"Are you sure? Because I could have sworn that I was doing exactly what your body was telling me you wanted."

Sitting up, she slides her garment over her head and then points at me.

"You may want to put that thing away before you open up the viewer."

I pull my pants back on, tucking my still half-hard erection inside. Then I lift her off the console and set her on her feet. She reaches up, pulling me back down only to lick her blood off my lips.

"You had a little something on you right there and thought I should help you out."

I start to grab her when she ducks out of the way, laughing and running through the door. If that light had not been flashing, I would have enjoyed nothing more than to chase her down for another round.

I hit the button for the viewer to engage, only to see EvO smiling on the other side, but he is looking everywhere but at me. He clears his throat.

"Good to see you made it back, big brother. Word of advice before we get started though, the next time you turn your viewer off, make sure the sound is off too!"

I lean my head down and rub my forehead while he laughs uncontrollably on the other side.

"I am going to assume the whole universe heard us?"

"Not the whole universe, just my flight crew. Once, I realized what or who was making all that ... sound ..." more laughter, "I turned it on mute! I figured you would notice the control panel blinking sooner or later."

"I am never going to live this down, am I?"

"Of course ... NOT! I cannot wait to tell AvX. But for now, I am here to save your ass. If you include that, you now have two things to live down. I am almost to your coordinates. You should be able to see me at any time."

I open the side viewer just as he comes into sight.

"That is one aggressive battlecruiser you are commanding there, little brother."

"I am proud of the old girl, and once we taught her our language, she gave up all her secrets. We even gave her a name to suit her purpose now; the Devastation. She and Falcor are two powerhouses few want to mess with. I will not be able to bring the Traveler on board, but we have plenty of room for the rest. Notify the other shuttle of our approach as I will come for it first. Let me know when it is ready and I will simply pull it into the docking bay. Your shuttle will be a little trickier, since you seem attached to something. Do we have any injuries or anything else I need to be concerned about?"

"No injuries that I am aware of. The cargo hold I am attached to contains all their belongings."

EvO nods his head. "I understand and get ready, once I grab hold of your shuttles, the ride may get a little bumpy. When I have you secured and on board, the crew has made rooms available for everyone and for once, you can sit back and relax for the next few risings and let me do the flying. Father already has the stealth shuttle ready to take you to the surface, as we are trying to keep grandfather's arrival a secret for a little while longer. I am glad I was close to home and will not miss out on the celebration of your and grandfather's return. I hope to have time to speak with him before we are all planet side, as I will never get a chance once Father is there."

"I am ready to sit in the passenger seat. Come get me, little brother."

CHAPTER 27

RAZ

I stare through the viewer, watching Darverius get closer and closer. This is a sight I was not sure I would ever get to see again over the last few orbital rotations or Katherine's years. I cannot wait to get planet side. I am ready to sleep in my own bed, hug my father, and start the rest of my life with my mate.

Ever since we docked with the Devastation, I have been lucky if I see Katherine for more than a few moments at a time. The holo comms in our room have been on nonstop. Between father and all my brothers, we have talked for so long I am losing my voice. Unfortunately, with the stealth shuttle docking at any time to pick us up, and with the celebration of our return, I will be lucky to see her at a distance once we land.

Father and grandfather have talked almost nonstop from the moment the holo screens were uplinked. I know grandfather has taken the time to talk to each of his grandsons because the ship is buzzing with conversations and excitement as we get closer to Darverius.

I even saw Katherine and Victoria talking to the other planetside human females earlier. The Traveler has remained offline and most of her systems are locked down so that there can be no further damage. EvO had the crew attach her to the main hull and he is currently towing her toward Falcor for SoL to do his magic.

The human boy Danny has been restless but still seems to be sleeping. His pup Raven has practically doubled in size overnight. Her glossy black coat and startling blue eyes are stunning in appearance. The other Hellhounds, even though they are twice her size and substantially older, seem to look to her for instructions and comfort. She may be smaller, but she seems to be surrounded by a blue aura that radiates power and dominance. It will be interesting to see how they mingle with my Selin.

I smell her as she tries to sneak up behind me. I twist at the last minute, grabbing her by the waist and throwing her up into the air like someone would a youngling. She grabs my arms as she lets out a small screech because I have surprised her. Ghost growls behind me until he hears her laughter. I catch her and pull her into me for a kiss before I set her back on the ground.

"Lord, RaZ, one of these days you're going to give me a heart attack."

. . .

"Can we play medic and the patient if I do?"

"You are insufferable, so it's a good thing you're so damn cute, or you would never get by with half the meanness you get up to!"

"Are you flirting with me, Miss?"

"Maybe? What do you plan on doing about it?"

Just as I bend down to whisper in her ear all the things I plan on doing to her the moment I have her alone, EvO's voice comes through the ship.

"Everyone proceed to the shuttle bay to head planetside."

"Come on, let's go, I want a seat next to the main ramp. If I do not stretch these wings out soon, we may as well have them taken off. All this walking is overrated!"

When the stealth shuttle lands, I am shocked that Father is not on it. I was sure he would come to pick us up. Everyone is smiling and they are all talking at once as we board the shuttle. I can see the relief on all their faces that we are finally here.

.   .   .

THE RAMP CLOSES AND I FEEL THE ENGINES POWER UP UNDER US. The stealth ship is pilotless as it has a direct link to Falcor, another one of SoL's many little creations. The ride is smooth and that makes it easier for me to point out the landmarks below. It honestly has me looking at Darverius like it is brand new. I shift from foot to foot as we land effortlessly on Father's mountaintop.

THE RAMP STARTS TO OPEN SLOWLY AND JUST WHEN IT IS ABOUT halfway open, I grab Katherine and shoot straight up into the sky. I can hear a gasp from the crowd below as we soar high above them. I twist and twirl playfully then head straight for the ground, my wings catching us effortlessly right before my feet touch the ground.

I OPEN MY WINGS UP, SET KATHERINE DOWN AND GRAB MY father in a huge hug. The feeling of his large, solid body holding me tightly makes it all worth it. His Symbots flare up and over my arms, hugging me back in their own way.

I STEP BACK, SHAKING MY WINGS OUT.

"FRACK, I NEEDED THAT! I WAS WORRIED THEY WOULD NOT EVEN work anymore. As the humans might say, the drive home was a bitch, Father!"

THE SOUND OF DEEP LAUGHTER HAS ME LOOKING AROUND. MY heart hits my throat when I see all of them. Every one of my brothers stands in a half circle surrounding Father. A rainbow of muscle and support as they all await the legend getting ready to walk down the ramp.

Katherine is laughing as she talks to Kira. I pull her away and position her in front of me. Then I take my place beside father turning to await grandfather's arrival.

CHAPTER 28
TYBERIUS

The ramp lowers all the way down and I step up to the edge. I can't believe after all these years, I'm finally back home. I'm scared to move forward, afraid that all of this is just a dream. I close my eyes and take a deep breath as familiar smells surround me.

Victoria grabs my hand and she doesn't say a word. She simply stands here beside me, giving me her support as I start to take that first step forward. The three hounds behind us growl when they notice everyone awaiting our arrival.

I hear Katherine whistle and they run down the ramp and immediately gather at her side, brushing against her lovingly.

I slowly walk down the ramp with my heart in my throat at the sight before me. Blood red tears flow down my cheeks as DaR and all my twenty-two grandsons await our arrival. My very legacy stands proudly before me.

I hear a soft voice ask, "Is that my other Papaw, Daddy?"

Then I watch in amazement as the little one squirms out of her daddy's arms and runs right up to me.

"Hi, me is Keida. I'm the da girl in dis famiry. Do you wants to be my Papaw too? Me heared a girl can never has too many!" She reaches her small arms up to me and I quickly pick her up.

She takes her little hand and wipes away the tears on my face. "Don't cry Papaw, dis bees a happy day!"

"Yes, my precious little one, it truly is." I kiss her on the cheek and set her back on her feet and watch as she runs back to XuL, who throws her up into the air before settling her back on his hip.

I have been lucky enough to talk to each of my grandsons over the last few rotations as we have gotten closer to Darverius. DaR and I could have spoken nonstop for months on end, and I would still feel like I missed out on most of his life. I couldn't be prouder of the man standing before me.

DaR takes the first step toward me, and I feel my legs start to run to him. No amount of hugs or tears could express my love for my only child.

My emotions are on overload as it finally dawns on me that I'm home. The Lord of Light never forgot me, even when I was at my lowest point. Me being here right now is the proof. I grab DaR close and sob. His familiar smell surrounds me as we stand here, simply holding each other. I have no idea how long we stand this way, and I don't care when suddenly, I feel someone small push their way in-between us.

"Me hugs toooo, Papaw."

DaR and I step back, and he reaches down to pick up the little one that called me papaw before.

"Dad, this little attention demander is Keida."

"Papaw, him already knows dat … me tells him." Her little arms reach out, pulling us back together.

"It was a reaaalllly long hug and me luvs hugs, dem are me favowites … so me wanted two Papaw huggies toooo. See? Dis is much more betterer."

I laugh at her innocence as I hear one of the females trying to coax her away from us.

"Keida, sweetheart, come here and meet everyone else. You are gonna have all kinds of new friends."

"Awww, but Papaw gives the best hugs."

"I know, baby."

"Opay, Papaw … me down. Mommy gonna make me goes do dumb girly tings!"

I can't hide the smile on my face when DaR sets her on her feet. We both watch her walk over to XuL and his mate Brittany, a pout on her face the whole way.

SoL must have seen this because he steps forward and lifts her up onto his massive shoulder. I see him whisper something to her and a huge smile suddenly forms on her face. SoL's mate rolls her eyes, laughing. Apparently, bribing a child is the same no matter the world you're on. He lifts his hand up, tickling her, and that's when I see the mark.

I look around at all the males in front of me stunned by what I'm seeing. Then I reach forward, taking DaR's large arm in my hand. I touch his Symbots and they part under my gentle touch as I trace the House of DaR mark on his arm.

Tears flow down my face and my heart hurts because I wasn't here to support him when he needed me the most.

"I had no idea, son. I should have known though ... it simply never crossed my mind. You have House status, something I have dreamed of obtaining for you throughout my career. There are no words to express how proud I am of you. You grew into a male that became so much more than I could have ever imagined or dreamed of, and I wasn't here to see it. I hate that I missed the day you were granted this honor."

"But you were Father, no matter the accomplishment or the failure. You were always with me. Your guidance and the standards that you instilled in me made me into the male I am today. Look out at your legacy and the males standing behind me. I understand how you feel, as I too am humbled by the honor our family has been bestowed.

Come, this rising we have been blessed beyond measure. Let us go greet the young ones who have awaited your arrival and then we will discuss reintroducing you back into society."

DaR introduces me to each one of his sons and if they are mated, I also meet their families. I was able to talk to each of them on board, but it is different seeing each one of them in person. I can't believe the years and the lives I have missed out on here, but I can't overlook the many blessings I received on Earth.

I look back at Victoria, happy to see her laughing with the other females. She must have sensed my stare because she looks up and smiles back at me. Knowing she is close helps me hold it all together. Even though everything should seem familiar, nothing does. I have been gone for so long, I'm the stranger here.

DaR's female claps her hands together.

"Can I get everyone's attention, please? If we could all move to the back of the house, SAGE has prepared a wonderful meal for everyone. This will be the first sit-down meal you have all been able to attend as one family, but don't think for a minute this will be the only one, boys. Ohhh, and the last one to the table only gets the leftovers!"

Some of the males start racing toward the dwelling like young ones. RaZ immediately launches into the sky, his large wings quickly overtaking the ones on the ground. I hear them all cheering and yelling at each other as RaZ calls them losers from above. He turns mid-race, only to come back to scoop Katherine off her feet, and then once again his powerful wings overtake the ones on foot.

I laugh at their antics. Victoria comes to my side, and I take her hand in mine. I raise it to my lips, kissing it and grateful for the silent strength she is providing to me right now. We start for the dwelling, hand in hand when a growl behind me has me turning back to the shuttle. Raven stands on the ramp, her blue eyes pulsing as she looks around at the unfamiliar landscape in front of her. Then I see a small head peeking around the edge of the ramp.

Victoria releases my hand and runs up the ramp. I see little Keida dart right up behind her. Raven growls when XuL follows and even snaps at him when he starts to reach down to pick Keida up.

"Daddy no!" I hear her say to XuL and I can tell it's taking everything he has not to grab her away from the massive, snarling animal in front of her. She holds her hand out to Raven.

"Yous such a pwetty girl ... is hers yours?"

We all move to the ramp, ready to jerk the child out of the way if Raven makes the first aggressive move against her. Instead, Raven stares at Keida, turning her head sideways, her blue eyes flashing red, and just as I see XuL reach his limit and patience, Raven goes down on one knee, bowing her head to the child in front of her.

I know I'm not the only one standing here with their mouth hanging open.

Raven rises back up and moves out of the way. Keida runs over to Danny. The poor little guy stands before her on wobbly legs, holding Victoria's hand.

Danny reaches out, running his hand through one of the pink strands of Keida's hair.

"You are absolutely beautiful," I hear him practically whisper. "Where am I?"

Keida's pink eyes swirl and dance mischievously. "Yous xactly where yous apposed to be, wis me!"

CHAPTER 29

RAZ

I don't think I have ever seen a table this big. Nor have I seen all my brothers in one place ever in my lifetime. Father said this was Kira's idea and that this family get-together was a common thing on Earth.

Grandfather sits at one end of the table and father on the other; all of his sons are sitting in the order of their birth along with the few of us that have mates.

I look around at the laughter surrounding me as my brothers tease and pick on each other. Even though very few of us resemble father in appearance, if I look closely enough, you can see him in all of us, from the way we hold ourselves, to our mannerisms.

I watch Katherine as she looks up and down the table.

Are you alright?"

"Yeah, and please don't take this wrong, but damn, I'm glad it was you I was meant to be with. Because if it had been the big green guy on the other end or even the massive one you all call SoL, I'm not sure if I would have come ... or if I would have run for my life."

I can't hold back my laughter. I stretch one of my wings around her from behind and pull her in close to me. Kissing her nose gently before I rub mine against hers, I say, "So, what you are saying is you like me best?"

"Well, don't let it go to your head, but yes. Some of your brothers kinda freak me out. Not including your dad. Damn! He's intense and he screams alpha male just standing over there with his arms crossed. You told me Kira softened him up some, so I can't imagine him being any more severe than he is now. The only time I can see any difference is when he looks at her. Even as tough as he is, he can't hide the love he has for her. XuL, I haven't figured out at all; he's just scary as shit. And I would hate to get on SoL's bad side, because if he grabbed you with those meat hooks of his, you're a goner.

And have you seen that huge, lizard-like thing sitting behind Kira? I damn near screamed my head off when it jumped on her shoulder earlier. I originally thought it was fake; its eyes don't even move, that's freaky. Apparently, Brittany has one too, and before you get any ideas about getting me one ... that is not my idea of a pet!"

"Oh, you're talking about the Uanas ... Ickis and Iggy. Ickis bonded with Kira shortly after she arrived here, which is very rare. They are extremely private and elusive animals, not to mention dangerous, but they have proved to be extremely loyal too. I watched Ickis cut down a Korgon like he was nothing while protecting Kira one time. They have massive blades hidden inside their tails and can spit a venom-like substance that will melt anything it touches. I prefer them to be on our side for sure."

The sound of a youngling's laughter has all of us turning toward Danny and Keida. Danny has a huge smile on his face. A face that is covered in what looks like some sort of food. He is laughing at Keida, whose whole face is also covered in this sticky substance. They are pushing food at each other, laughing as it smears all over their faces and hands.

"Food fight!" I hear grandfather say and in utter shock, I watch as he throws some sort of soft tuber at Victoria. It hits her on her cheek and instead of her getting mad, she just smiles as she takes her finger, flicking it off, then she reaches over to the middle of the table and grabs a piece of bread. Then she throws it at him, hitting him right in the face. That's all it takes for pure pandemonium to break out. Every type of food imaginable is being thrown all over the room. I sit back laughing at everyone else and the mess they are making until something hits me in the chest. Horrified, I look down at the thing slowly sliding down my belly.

Looking up, I try to figure out who did this when I see Katherine put her hand over her mouth, trying not to laugh.

"Oh My God! If you could have seen your face the moment that hit you."

"You think this is funny, young lady? Well, let me share."

I take a chunk of blob off my lap and smear it all over her face only to hear Ghost growl. Apparently, he has been lying under the table at her feet this whole time. Unconsciously, her eyes flash a bright blue and before I can react, she dumps her whole plate on my head.

I hear my father yell out. "Sons ... Males ... Children ... Father! For the love of the Lord of Light, they have all gone mad!"

We all must have heard him at the same time because every dish left on the table goes sailing his way. He manages to duck a few of them but in no time, he is covered. Father stands with his arms out, food dripping off every inch of him. The look on his face is priceless. Kira is hiding behind his large frame, laughing so hard she is practically crying. I watch as she runs a finger across his belly, rubbing a random piece of food off him. She then sticks it in her mouth, smacking her lips as if it were delicious.

I see him look down at her with a scowl on his face, until he sees her laughing at him. He picks her up against him, rubbing his now food covered body all over her.

"NOOO, DaR I was still clean!" We all laugh as she tries to escape his massive arms.

Finally, everyone settles down, but not one of us managed to escape the mess. I watch in awe as the large table starts to sink into the floor and the food simply disappears with it.

SAGE's voice booms through the entire room.

"That will be the last time I work for half a rising to set a table for all of you heathens, as Kira would say. Stand up, all of you! I will run an ionizer over you all at once."

I see Keida grab Danny's arm, trying to sneak outside when SAGE stops her.

"Miss Keida, don't even think about walking out of this room, young lady. You started this fiasco, and I would prefer the rest of my dwelling not to be covered in your stickiness."

We watch as Keida whispers something to Danny, both of them laughing. She turns her head and I watch her beautiful eyes widen in sudden fear. Before I even think about it, I launch myself at her and Danny, snatching both of them up in my arms. They grab me around the neck as I turn in a crouch, my claws out, ready to destroy whatever has scared her.

I hear my brothers draw their weapons and then SoL's massive form is standing in front of us, protecting not only me, but the children. I hear Raven roar out a warning before she and a young Selin run into the room, both of them immediately coming to my side, snarling at the unknown threat in the room.

Keida is shaking like a leaf in my arms, but I see nothing in the room that could have scared her. SoL turns to reach for her. I release her only to pull Danny closer, rubbing his back gently.

"Keida, honey tell Unka SoL what's wrong."

She has her head tucked into his neck and if I hadn't been standing right behind them, I may not have heard her. She points over to the corner, "Dem shadows is movin by dem themselfs."

Out of the corner of my eye, I see father jump across the remaining chairs, his hand grabbing something out of the shadowy corner.

Maniacal laughter echoes across the room, as father pulls a male out of the dark corner holding him by his neck. Father shakes him roughly. "Who are you? How did you get into this dwelling? How dare you enter this home?"

The male smiles a smile that hints at his cruelty. His eyes glow an eerie yellow out of a face that could be my father's twin. "I am your SSSiiiNNN ... I thought all your sons were welcome here, after all, it is a celebration! What is this confused look on your face, **Father**? Do you see a ghost standing before you?"

He knocks Father's hand off his neck and simply fades away into a dark mist. The echo of his crazed laughter slowly leaves the room.

I have no idea how that thing ... that male could have broken loose of Father's hold, or how he simply faded away like that.

Danny's bottom lip is trembling, and Keida is still softly crying in SoL's arms. Then everyone starts talking at once.

"Silence!" Father yells out and Danny jerks in my arms.

"SAGE, how did that ... that male, get past our sensors?"

"Commander, I have no idea. I personally checked every male myself upon entry into the main dwelling. My program would have instantly detained anything or anyone without your genetics. Hold for one moment while I look over something."

"He looked like my evil twin, SAGE. That was no youngling, that was a full-grown male that has either had his features changed or ..." I watch him run a hand through his hair. "Lord of Light can it be possible ... is he one of mine?"

"Commander, the sensors picked up an oddity only moments before Miss Keida saw the intruder. It looks like there were twenty-five males in the room instead of twenty-four. You, your father, your twenty-two sons and that male. He has the same molecular structure as all of you. His genetic markers were actually higher than those of any of your other sons. Technically, if he would have been brought to your attention sooner, he would be number twenty-three. Commander, he seems to have an almost identical physiology as you. There is no mistaking it, this male is ninety-nine percent yours."

Kira walks up behind father, rubbing his back gently as he stands there with his head down. "How could this have happened?" I hear him saying to no one in particular.

Keida squirms out of SoL's grasp and heads straight to father. He picks her up and is forced to look at her when she puts both of her hands on his face. "Papaw, hims was a bad man, hims not like you."

Father kisses her on the cheek and hands her over to Kira, who bounces her on her hip, squeezing her tight. I can hear her talking softly to Keida, telling her how brave she was, and to always tell us if she sees the bad man.

"SAGE, set all programs to notify me if his signature reappears anywhere on our scanners."

"Confirmed. I have notified Falcor, and SCOUT as well."

Footsteps have us all turning, weapons drawn again. Tordan enters the room and puts his hands up when he sees all of us ready for battle.

"Hey, I'm the good guy, remember. I knew I was going to be late, but do we always have to resort to violence boys?"

Everyone drops their weapons as he walks toward me, his arms stretched out as he hugs me and Danny both at the same time.

"Good to see you, son. It looks like I have missed out on all the excitement."

"Never a dull moment in this dwelling for sure. Tordan, it's good to see you."

"Who is this little male?"

"This is Danny, we brought him with us. I figured we could use a couple more warriors to watch over Miss Keida."

Danny reaches out hesitantly, touching Tordan's mechanical arm. "You're a terminator."

"I can be, little man."

Keida suddenly appears. "Tordy, did you comes to play wit me and SeeSee, ohhh and Danny toos? Der was a bad shadow man but Papaw chaseded him all gone!"

"That Papaw of yours is good at that. Let me talk to him for a moment and then you can finally introduce me to your SeeSee."

"Opay! Come on Danny, let's go plays in the garden. You gots to see the magcal buggies dat likes to pay on da water. Mommy say thems be soooo cool!"

I set Danny down. Tordan and I are watching the kids run out of the room when Grandfather yells out his name and then grabs him, hugging him tightly.

"Tordan, my chosen second son! I was wondering when you were going to show up. Look at you, over there trying to impress the females with those arms of yours. I'm happy to see you have adjusted well to it; when you were a youngling, you did your best to hide it."

Tordan flexes his mechanical arm. "It has served me well Tyberius, father of my heart. It is good to see you back where you belong. Many a rising we could have used your wisdom and guidance. When things calm down, I would enjoy spending an early darkness together, and possibly a meal. I have missed your calming presence in our world, but as always, something needs my immediate attention, and I need to speak to DaR. Then it looks like I have a play-date with the best-looking female here."

"I look forward to it my second son, I can't wait for you to tell me about your other enhancements. Also, we need to get the females translators as soon as possible. I'm assuming you are the male in charge of that."

"Once you have rested, I will have SAGE provide them for you. She has a highly advanced medical center on premises and can do the procedure effortlessly."

Grandfather hugs Tordan once again. I hear him whisper, "May the Lord of Light guide you on your next adventure and Tordan, follow your heart."

Someone yells out grandfather's name and he turns away from, us heading outside.

"Come on Tordan, I will go that way with you. I need to tell Father I am headed home. Then I plan on running off with the other best-looking female here."

Father sees us approaching, "Father, I am going to leave now. I have a whole world to show Katherine. We will be in touch in a few risings unless you need me sooner."

"I believe I have this newest problem handled, son ... for now anyway. You take your female and enjoy yourselves. I will rest easier just knowing you are home."

Father grabs me again, hugging me tightly. When he lets go of me, he says, "We will talk in a few rotations."

He turns from me, grabbing Tordan by the arm. "Tordan, I was wondering if you were going to be able to make it. What was the holdup this time?"

"I was getting ready to release my station to come here when a report came in that caught my eye. You know we stripped the Destroyer of all records, and I had a program running in the background this whole time to see if we could possibly find out what happened to the other human females that were on board Kira and Brittany's ship? I believe I may have found one on Targres Four. I request permission to head there now. I plan on doing a reconnaissance mission to see if the reports are even accurate first. If I manage to locate the female, I will comm you to see how you wish to proceed."

"Absolutely, go Tordan. All I ask is that you leave your personal comm on at all times. I do not want to run into another situation like SoL's. I also want updates every darkness. If I have not hear from you, I will come."

"I would expect nothing less, DaR. SAGE informed me on the flight down what occurred here. Is it possible that you could have had another son, DaR? I know we do not speak of it, but if this male truly looks like you and the genetics match the way SAGE says they do, then there is no other answer. If the male was raised on that planet ... Well, I do not need to tell you how unstable he is then. Especially when he sees the opportunities your other offspring were granted from birth. You need to tell Kira. The last thing you need is for her to hear this from someone else."

"Yes, yes ... I will do that as soon as I get it to make sense in my head. It seems like our past will forever haunt us. Please be careful out there Tordan, Targres Four can be as dangerous as it is beautiful."

CHAPTER 30
RAZ

"You ready to ditch this joint?"

"What was that? Have you been hiding your knowledge of Earth-slang from me?"

"Well ... I heard so much of it when I was gathering all the space satellites to try to find Earth that I think it started to sink in. Then being around all my brothers with human mates, father, grandfather and you, and I think it will start slipping out more!

Now, I was going to give you time to tell everyone goodbye, but we would never get out of here, so how good are you at sneaking around?"

"I can hold my own, but I'm not the one hauling around ten-foot wings. But what about Uncle Ty and Vic?"

"They are going to stay here for a few risings. Father still has not announced his return, so they have many things to work through before grandfather can be reintroduced into society. It will be good for Victoria to be around the other females too."

"I'm assuming you plan on keeping me all to yourself?"

"For a little while yes, since they have had you all to themselves for your whole life. I need some me-and-you time, but if you are not ready to go..."

"Nope, as you just said ... let's ditch this joint!"

I reach out to take her hand and slowly start making our way outside. I hear Katherine whistle for her hounds the moment we clear the door, and I launch us straight up into the air; her laughter and mine mingling together. I lower us closer to the ground when I see her hounds following us. I land at the border of my Dark Forest and father's wall that encloses his dwelling.

Katherine stands in front of me, looking around until her hounds catch up. "Wow, RaZ, talk about culture shock. I don't believe there is a single thing the same here as on Earth. I mean, if you really need a serious reality check, just look up. That Saturn-looking planet is practically on top of our heads. And what is the big black thing floating in the sky?"

"That thing you are calling Saturn is one of our three moons, with that one in particular being Sybrus One. It is a major trade center for the whole galactic region. The large black object is Solanar, and was Darverius' first defense center, and now it's mostly used by the elite. I stopped here because I wanted you to see this doorway. If, for some reason, you decide to walk here, this is the only entrance back into Father's dwelling. SAGE monitors the walls at all times, but you will have no issues getting through. Are you ready to step into my world?"

"I guess I'm as ready as I'll ever be."

"Stay here for a tic and let me tell my queen Selin, Ola, about you; she is extremely territorial."

"How do you know she's here? I don't hear anything?"

"That's how I know she is here. She is watching us from the other side. All the other animals stay away from the Selin, especially a Queen. To be honest, I'm a little worried about how she will react to your hounds."

Ghost must have sensed something because he walks between RaZ and me, pushing me back away from the wall. The hair on his back is standing straight up as a deep growl leaves his throat. Thorn is also growling, his long fangs dripping venom on the ground below him. Glory pushes her way in front of them both, her body seeming to be growing even larger and is now pulsing all over in blue, lightning-like streaks.

Katherine shrugs, as we have no idea what to do now. Ola takes that decision from us. She simply walks through the force field and right to me. She is still larger than the hounds but not by much. Glory doesn't make a sound, and she doesn't move either when Ola passes within a few feet of her.

Ola nudges me affectionately, but she never takes her eyes off what she considers intruders. I try to send her an image showing her that they are friends. She sends me back an image of them all laying in pieces in front of her. I force myself to stop the laughter bubbling up in my throat because I don't want to give her the wrong idea. I walk over to Glory, putting my hand in front of her, and then I do the same to Ola.

Ola doesn't like me being that close to the other female. She uses her head to push me back.

Katherine steps past Ghost but stays behind Glory. "Ok, this isn't going to work, RaZ. Both females are looking for a weakness in the other. They are determined to tear each other apart. They are both alpha females and apparently, they are both fighting over you."

"Me?"

"Yeah, it seems you are overly popular with the girls, so I'm going to fix this. There is only room for one dominant female in your life and that's me."

I almost grab her when she walks between the two massive animals. Ola's head is level with Katherine's shoulders, and she could rip her head off before I could even react. Katherine's eyes flash red, then blue as she stares down at Ola. Glory backs off, standing between Ghost and Thorn. Ola takes a step forward and this is when I see a pale blue light surround Katherine.

Ola snarls and just as I start to step between them, Katherine puts her hand out to stop me. Ola starts sending me the images Katherine is showing her, but she doesn't back down until Katherine shows her the inner fire inside of her. The one I thought was extinguished. Ola lowers her head and steps back, nudging me before she turns and heads back inside the dark forest.

"Does this mean you guys are friends now? Or do we need to move?"

"She will be wary of us for a while, but in time, I believe she will warm up to the hounds and me. She will tell the other Selin of us, and from what I could tell from her chaotic thoughts, so long as she senses your happiness, we are welcome here."

I smile when I realize what she just said. "So, in other words, you must be on your best behavior. No *RaZ pick up your garments* ... or what do the men in your world call it ... *honey do list*? Yes, that is what it is. I don't want any of those either. I can see why your males got angry when handed one of those."

"RaZ, how in the world did you hear of a ... honey-do list?"

"I saw it on what you call TV shows, and they were on a satellite."

"I'm scared to ask what else you saw. Are we walking or flying the RaZ express?"

I spank her lightly. "Looks like I'm going to have to put that smart mouth of yours to work." I cup her cheeks in my hands and bend down, kissing her gently. "That's better! You know I'm not a huge fan of all this walking, but this time I believe you will appreciate it better from the ground. Come, I want you to see our home."

I grab her hand as we walk through the entrance to my world.

CHAPTER 31
KATHERINE

I take two steps forward and walk into a whole other world. The air is cool on my skin where the huge, dark trees block the sun's rays. I have always been one of the lucky ones because of my mixed heritage that the sun has never bothered me, but also because of that legacy, I have always been more comfortable in the dark.

I see the tension leaving RaZ's whole body as we walk hand in hand through what he calls his dark forest. I understand why it would seem terrifying to some. Especially with the Selin walking silently all around us. Glory is walking in front of RaZ, and my shadow Ghost is walking at my side. I lay my hand on his back, comforting him and myself at the same time.

The forest isn't as dark as it appeared when I first walked in, most of the plants are simply darker in color. Vines seem to wrap around the majority of the tree's trunks. I stop to watch a small dark purple flower open and close, almost as if they are breathing ... weird. I'm lost in my own thoughts, mesmerized by the sights around me and I'm not watching where I'm going when I bump into RaZ's back. His wings block my view of what is in front of us.

He pulls me forward and I gasp at the sight before me. A mammoth stone fortress stands in front of us. The black granite-looking rock sparkles like diamonds where the sunlight breaks through the trees. The walls are so shiny, they reflect the ground and skies above it, making it practically invisible.

"What do you think?"

"It's amazing! It looks like you took the blueprints of every castle on Earth and mixed them all together."

"It is not as large as it appears; the reflection stones it's built out of make it seem more than it is. From here it looks like it has multiple towers, but it only has one. It will look completely different from the inside. Come on."

Suddenly feeling nervous, I pull my hand out of his. "RaZ, wait a minute, I need a minute before we go any further. Can we stop and talk? Everything is moving so fast, and I am suddenly having a hard time catching up."

He turns toward me. "Forgive me, Katherine. I have been so caught up in our survival that I never took the time to ask you if you were alright. You seemed to pick yourself up right after that near disaster on the ship. Then after that, it seems like it's been one thing after another. I'm sorry, I should have given you more time for you to adjust."

"RaZ, you aren't wrong about the rollercoaster we have been on and I'm not saying that I'm not happy we are finally here, but it's all so overwhelming. I mean honestly, we barely know each other. Thank God you're hot. That certainly helps the situation, so please don't take this the wrong way because this isn't about you. I want you to know that I think you're over the top gorgeous, you're funny, and you seem to be extremely sweet and caring. But my head is swimming with all that's happened to us, and I'm terrified of what's going to happen next. I haven't had time to get used to anything before the next new thing comes along, let alone process the fact that we are a couple. And don't give me that look, I'm not saying that's a bad thing, but damn, RaZ. Look at this from my point of view. I'm on an alien planet that has two suns and three moons, not to mention the other weird floaty things hovering above us. Your family looks like a rainbow on steroids. For god's sake, the freaking house talked RaZ ... that shit ain't normal! Let's not forget that we almost died only days from reaching your home because of a rogue AI. I couldn't make up a story this crazy and I'm one more thing away from flipping the hell out!!"

"Katherine, we have an eternity to get to know each other, so you need to quit pushing yourself so hard. On a lighter note, you're the alien now ... does that make you feel better?"

"Nope, not really."

"I promise, things will calm down, and then you will have all the time in the world to put everything into perspective."

"I guess seeing the house you plan on us living in made it a reality and that hit me hard. I just realized I'm not in Kansas anymore, and you have the rainbow family to prove it. Lord RaZ, what if this all backfires on us, and somehow or someday you are disappointed and regret coming for me? Do you realize how much pressure that puts on a girl? It's not like I can go back home if we don't work out."

He gently grabs my arms, making me look up at him. "Ok, you are making problems that are not there. Your mind and the things you have been put through are making you your own worst enemy. We have overcome extremes that have put us right here, right in this moment where we're supposed to be. We will fight, we will argue, and that's ok! We are different beings. We are not expected to see everything the same. All I can promise you is that I will never go to bed without kissing you good night, nor will I ever want another. You are stuck with me, do you understand?"

"Yeah, but what if you squeeze the toothpaste from the middle, or you leave all the cabinet doors open? What if you drink the milk straight out of the container? Or even worse ... you leave the commode seat up!"

I can tell this was not what he expected me to say. "I'm at a loss as to what this tooth of paste is, so that won't be a problem. All the cabinets will automatically shut themselves, so mark that one out. I don't drink anything but blood, and yes, I will take it straight from the tap, whether that's from you or a bag. Now this commode thing, because of my wings, my elimination units have been customized. If they're not something you like, we will install your own. Has this put all the silliness of that very big, over-imagination of yours to rest?"

"I'm overthinking it, aren't I?"

"No, there is no such thing. Don't you think there are things that I'm worried about, too? I mean, what if I can't provide you with the things you need? Will you ever truly be happy here away from everything you have ever known? What if you snore? Or what if your cooking is so bad I'll be scared to enter the kitchen?"

"You hardly eat any solid food, RaZ."

"Ohh well, then scratch that last one off too. Now, are you ready to be ravished until you can no longer think about anything?"

"Are you the one offering this service?"

"I think I'm up for it, yes."

"Well, what are you waiting for? Lead the way, Master Ravisher."

"Ooo, I like that title ... will you call me that from now on?"

"I have to be ravished first to see if you're worthy."

The whole time we have been play-arguing, RaZ has been leading me toward the front door. He lays his hand against it and the door simply disappears. "Nice trick." He steps away from me as I walk forward, looking up. When he said the inside looked completely different, he wasn't lying.

The whole place is a huge tower with a massive stairway that encircles the walls from the floor to the top. A top that I can barely see from here. Doorways, or I should say giant archways seem to shoot off in every direction. The walls glisten in pale shades of blue and green. Openings above us shimmer, casting their colors throughout like I'm turning a toy kaleidoscope.

"Is that look on your face good or bad?"

"Wow, RaZ, this is amazing, I would've never imagined anything like this." I walk in a circle trying to see everything.

"I built this myself. I have never liked conventional dwellings as my wings are usually too large for most of them or for me to fit comfortably. The open center here makes it easy for me to fly from one place to another. As you know, I'm not a huge fan of all this walking you all do so much of. When I first built it, there was no stairway at all. I didn't personally need them, so I put my efforts elsewhere. That is until my brothers started showing up. When I had to fly SoL's big ass up because he wanted a tour of the place, I began the stairs the next day."

"I can't imagine how long this took to build, and you did it all?"

"All me. I laid every stone and cut every piece of wood. I even designed most of the furniture, which was made specifically to fit each room. And as to how long it took to build, well I have never really stopped."

"So, what you're saying is not only are you cute, but you're handy too, and your primary goal in life is to excel as a master seducer? I think you are a man after my own heart."

He grabs me around the waist, and I wrap my arms around his neck as I feel my feet leave the ground.

"I will be your only seducer, do you understand? I won't share."

"That's ok, I don't share well either. I blame it on being an only child, as I never had to share my toys and I got all the attention. It was a win-win for me."

"No, what it means is that you are used to getting your way."

"Yeah, that's probably it too. Does this place have a bedroom?"

When I feel my feet touch the ground, I look over my shoulder. Unwinding my arms from his neck, I turn to look at the room we just entered. The room smells like RaZ, and as I walk in, I take a deep breath, breathing him in. There is probably the largest bed I have ever seen sitting on a platform in the middle of the room and it is decorated beautifully in dark burgundies and browns. I walk toward a window and peer down at the ground far below us. I can see RaZ's Selin walking around the perimeter. My own Hellhounds lay in front of the house. I guess I should find them another name now, as we have all changed into something else.

I hear RaZ behind me and just as I start to turn, something catches my eye. I lean up against the window and stare out at what appears to be a female wearing a long white dress. The veil is so long that it's floating beyond the tree line. She turns to me and even though her face is concealed by the veil, I know she is looking up at me. I press my hand against the window, but I don't feel anything from her like I always have from the other lost souls that have besieged me my whole life. She doesn't feel dead, she feels absent. Like her soul is here, but her body is somewhere else.

She hovers above the ground, looking back at me for another minute then she turns, floating off into the distance.

"RaZ, do spirits come to rest in your dark forest?"

"Why did you see our fabled princess?"

"I saw something. I tried to reach out to her, but it didn't feel like she was in the in-between; she feels here. I'm not sure how that's possible."

RaZ wraps his arms around me from behind as we both look out over the forest below. "I have lived in this forest for most of my life, and I have never seen her. You are here for a few minutes, and she pops up. As you humans would say ... go figure. What do you want to do? Are you tired? Hungry? Would you enjoy a long bath?"

"Is this bath big enough for two?"

"I think we can make it work."

"Then a bath it is."

"Don't go anywhere, I will be right back."

"I don't have anywhere else to go," I whisper to no one.

CHAPTER 32

RAZ

I feel bad. I have been so focused on getting us home, I didn't think about the major traumas Katherine has been through. I could kick myself for not paying more attention to her. This whole time, she has been fun and teasing, but now I can see it's all just been an act. It was simply her way of dealing with the things going on around her. She owns my heart and I hate to see her hurting like this. I look back at her as she stares out the window and she looks so lost.

I enter the bathing room I installed just off my sleeping chamber. This room probably took me longer to build than all the others combined because I kept changing the layout. I'm glad now that I decided to make the main tub larger. I push a button on the wall, and the floor starts to retract, revealing the large sunken pool beneath it. Its steam rises, quickly filling up the space.

. . .

"I'M READY WHEN YOU ARE," I YELL OUT AS I YANK OFF MY BOOTS and then pull off my pants and vest. Taking everything off feels so good that I may never wear clothes again. I walk down the built-in steps, moaning as I lower myself down into the hot water. My wings stretch out, floating weightlessly in the water behind me. My muscles relax for the first time in what feels like forever. I close my eyes, my mind drifting off reliving the years I was gone. There were so many times I didn't think I was going to make it back. And if this is a dream, or if I'm dead, but in this dream world I'm home, and I got the girl ... just leave me here.

I OPEN MY EYES JUST IN TIME TO SEE HER EMERGE THROUGH THE mist in the room. Her small feet don't make a sound on the floor as she walks toward me. "Be careful, the floor will be slick."

SHE STANDS BEFORE ME COMPLETELY DRESSED EXCEPT FOR HER shoes. "You look like a winged god sitting there stretched out like that, RaZ."

"I LIKE THE SOUND OF THAT. IF YOU WANT ME TO REMAIN HERE, I believe I will need a sacrifice."

"Ohh, now you're a demanding God! What is it you want, my Lord?"

"I WANT A CURVY, EBONY-HAIRED, BLUE-EYED TEMPTRESS ... WITH skin so soft it's like caressing silk."

· · ·

"That's a big order. I will see what I can come up with."

She acts like she is going to turn away from me, and I lunge for her, dragging her into the water clothes and all. She comes out of the water sputtering and spitting as the water drips down her face. Before she can say a word, I bend down, capturing her lips with mine, deepening it only when I feel her slide her hands up into my hair pulling me closer. One thing I will never have to worry about is this explosive passion and want between us.

I grab both sides of her shirt and simply rip it apart. As I lower my head, I take one of her perfect breasts into my mouth. She gasps as I take my tongue, flicking her nipple gently until it tightens into a hard peak. Then I bite down, barely breaking the skin as I pull the very essence that is Katherine inside of me.

Lifting her up I lick my way down her stomach stopping only long enough to circle my tongue around her belly button. I leave little love bites on her side as I work her pants off her legs.

Once I have her completely naked and in my arms, I pull my wings around and they grasp her arms pulling her upper body away from me, as I maneuver her lower body directly in front of my face. I can see her natural juices coating her lower lips. I grasp her hips, pulling her forward ... it is time to feast.

. . .

I withdraw my claws so that I won't accidentally cut her and insert two of my long fingers inside her, slowly moving them in and out as I suck on this precious little pleasure nub of hers. Every moan and gasp leaving her lips as she squirms in front of me presses me on. I remove my fingers only to insert my tongue inside of her. Consuming her natural nectar, my body suddenly feels high from the potency of her blood and natural juices now flowing through my own system.

She screams out my name as her body crests in passion. I don't give her a moment to come down before I'm standing up, thrusting deep inside of her. She claws at me, shouting RaZ and it takes everything I have to hold still, giving her time to adjust to my size.

I pull her body up against mine, enjoying the feel of her breasts rubbing against my chest. At some point, I've stopped being able to think. All I can do is feel when Katherine peaks once more. I can no longer hold back as her walls milk my shaft. My legs are suddenly so weak I practically fall back into the water.

She pushes her hair out of her face and within seconds we are both laughing. "Good thing we don't have neighbors huh?"

"I was that good, right?"

"No, absolutely terrible ... like the worst ever."

. . .

"I'LL DO BETTER NEXT TIME."

THE SMILE ON HER FACE MAKES MY HEART FLUTTER AS I HOLD ALL that is dear to me here in my arms. "Come on, let's go sleep for at least a rotation."

"THAT SOUNDS WONDERFUL, BUT I THINK I'M TOO WEAK TO walk."

"NOW MY HEAD IS SWELLING; NOTHING LIKE KNOWING YOU'VE exhausted your woman so well she can't move afterward." I can't help but laugh when she rolls her eyes at me.

PULLING HER CLOSE, I WALK UP THE STEPS THEN OVER TO THE wall, hitting the button for the ionizer to dry us off.

KATHERINE DOESN'T SAY A WORD, SHE SIMPLY TUCKS HER HEAD into my chest. When I pull her to me tightly, I swear I feel a tear run down my chest. I'm at a loss as to how to comfort her. I feel like there is nothing I can say or do to make this any easier.

LOWERING US DOWN ON THE BED, I TUG THE BLANKETS THAT Kira had sent me up and over our heads, cocooning us in our own little world. I wipe the tears she is trying to hide from me off her cheek. "Do you want to talk? I hate these tears, baby, it makes me feel helpless."

"To be honest Raz, I don't know why I'm crying. My mind is just so tired, if that makes sense? We ... I, have lost so much, but now I have you and this whole new world to explore and get used to. This has been the biggest adventure of my life and I'm so grateful to be here with you. You should know that I have never felt safer or more cared for than I do right now, but I just can't help thinking how much Mom would have loved all of this.

You don't know how many times she and Dad have crossed my mind on this journey. I don't know how to feel right now, and I know that's ok, but ... just hold me. I don't want to think right now. I simply want to enjoy you."

I kiss her forehead and tuck her in close, relieved when I finally feel her body relax into sleep.

CHAPTER 33
KATHERINE

The bed moving has me opening my eyes. I watch RaZ walk toward the archway in our bedroom, his large wings flaring out as he steps off the platform. I rub my eyes as I stretch my legs out, smiling when I hear him singing to himself below.

My mind feels lighter this morning. I have no idea how long we've slept, but I needed every minute of it. I grab the top blanket off the bed and walk to the window, looking out over the forest below. Thorn and Ghost are playing tug of war with a stick as Glory barks playfully around them.

They are the same, but so much different from what they were before. It's like the rage that was always inside of them, and inside of me, is gone. But it's been replaced by something else, something far more dangerous, yet calmer at the same time. I don't understand the changes taking place inside of me, but one thing I have learned in all these years is all things are answered with time. It will reveal itself to me when it's supposed to.

A whistle from the archway has me turning. "Frack, woman you are stunning! Do you know how hard it's going to be for me to leave you when I know this is what's waiting at home for me?"

His words hit me unexpectedly hard. "I take it you are going to have to leave." I can feel the tears coming and I look back out the window so he doesn't see me fighting them.

"Father and Tordan are blowing me up about the mission. Normally we would have met immediately after my return for a debriefing, but they knew I needed to get you settled first. I've been lucky they gave me these last few rotations without breaking our door down.

Father just contacted me saying that he is sending a shuttle down from Falcor shortly. SoL has also been working on the Traveler, and I hope to have some good news about ANDI to give to grandfather on my return. I thought that maybe after our breakfast, you might enjoy visiting Victoria while I was gone. She has been asking about you."

I can't keep the quiver out of my voice, and I can tell he heard it. "How long do you think you'll be gone?"

RaZ is beside me in two steps. He turns me around to face him and I put my head down, looking at the floor and trying to hide these tears. *What is wrong with me? I have never been this emotional.*

"Hey, none of this, please. I will only be gone half a rising or so, and if you don't want me to go, I will have them come here instead. You are way more important than their curiosity, or their questions about what happened to me in the last five and a half orbital rotations, or years as you call them. They have waited this long and they can just wait a little longer if need be."

I put my hand on his chest, focusing on its contours as I run my fingers over them. "No, RaZ, I'm being silly. Of course, I would like to see Vic and the other girls. I'm sorry, I had a clingy moment there. You will have to be patient with me. My emotions seem to be all over the place."

"Let me comm Father back and put this off. I don't like leaving you like this."

"I know you have responsibilities and a job here. I will be fine. Anyway, my curiosity is killing me about Kira and the others."

"Are you sure?"

"Yup!"

"Before I leave, I want you to try something. Now, it's an acquired taste, but it is the reason we originally got fangs according to the ancient text. Come here, I want you to try a Blood Beet."

He hands me a small plum-looking fruit and I hold it up to my nose, sniffing it. I try to squeeze it, but it's hard as a rock. "Is this ripe? Because I can see us losing a few teeth on this thing."

"Here let me show you, see this seam ... sink one of your fangs right here, like this."

I watch him sink a single fang into the Blood Beet. It takes me a few tries to get it right, but finally, I'm able to gain access to this famous fruit of theirs. RaZ drains several of them before I finish my first. The moment the juice inside of it is gone, it withers like a dried-up prune. It tastes like ... rum, without the alcohol. After having a few of them, I'm glad that I can eat solid foods because you are either going to like this thing or hate it.

"You don't have any A negative, or O positive on tap anywhere, do you?"

"I take it you don't care for it?"

"Let's just say I now understand why you were starving as a baby."

He shakes his head, laughing, "Come on, I believe I have a whole warmer full of yummies. It may not be the A negative you are used to, but we will find something you like. If not, you can always use me as a snack."

"I don't mind chewing on you, but unless it's a case of "have to", I've always preferred my dinners to be in a glass or a container." Before he can say anything back, I hear a beep coming from his personal comm.

"That's the shuttle alerting me that it just touched down. Get dressed and I will take you down to XuL's before I head up. I believe that's where grandfather and Victoria have been staying."

"It won't take me but a second; well, on second thought, it might. I have no clothes here RaZ, and I don't think I can wear this blanket." I hold out the sides, flashing him my naked skin for a second before I fold it back over me.

He growls playfully. "This lushness was made for my eyes only so it's a good thing that Victoria sent some of your belongings over the last darkness. I had the house bots put away what they could. Come here, let me show you."

He picks me up, biting my neck playfully as he walks across the room. Then I see him put his hand down on a stand and the wall disappears in front of us. Now that I'm paying attention, I can see scanners in the walls and on certain pieces of furniture. Apparently, there are things, or I should say possible rooms hidden everywhere. "What do you think?"

I haven't been paying as much attention to the room as I was the sensors, but when I look up, I'm speechless. "RaZ is this a closet?"

"Yes, slash safe. That's why it has a scanner on its doorway. Not only do I store my garments in here, but it also holds all my weapons and other things of value."

"Lord, RaZ! Honey, this room is bigger than some people's homes. Did you design this?"

"No, I stole the design from AvX. He is the most organized being in the whole universe. Everything must be in its place and in perfect working order at all times or he flips the hell out, as you would say."

"Yeah, I can see OCD all over this place. Give me a minute to grab something, then I'll be ready."

"Don't take that blanket off yet or we will never leave this dwelling. Oh, I also had all the scanners updated last darkness with your bio-signature, so now you will have access to everything."

"I notice your house doesn't talk like your father's."

"No, I didn't install an AI in the house when I was building it. I have always been very private even as a youngling. So, I knew when I started to build this dwelling that I wanted it completely self-sustainable and not hooked into a grid anywhere. If I had an AI unit, they would be in constant contact with all the others and I really didn't want that at the time, but now that you are here, the added security is something I am considering."

"I'm not helpless, RaZ. I'm a little more than the human girls your father and brother are involved with."

"You may be, but you are still mine to take care of and you shouldn't have to worry about any harm coming to you at all, especially in your own home."

I hear RaZ's comm go off again. "Oh, hell's fire, tell your dad to keep his pants on, we're coming!"

CHAPTER 34
KATHERINE

Our feet no more than touch the ground when RaZ kisses me quickly and then turns, launching back into the sky. I smile as I watch him twist and turn in the wind currents.

"You really can't beat his form of transportation."

"If it was up to him, I would never walk again." I turn to look at the pretty young girl standing beside me.

"Brittany, right?"

"I wasn't sure if you would remember. You kinda got bombarded when you guys landed."

"The girls were easy to remember, it was all the rainbow-colored studs I can't recall."

"OMG, that's the perfect description for all of them! Come on in, Victoria is busy making us some tea while Kira works on some snacks. I volunteered to come get you when the sensors notified me that you guys were here. If you don't mind, I need to check on

Keida before we head out to the atrium. Did RaZ give you any history about this place?"

"All he said was this was the family home."

"This is where Tyberius raised DaR, and in turn, DaR raised his oldest sons here."

"I have so many questions."

"Hopefully, I can help with some of those. If not, we always have SAGE ... she knows everything."

"That's the house, right?"

"SAGE is more like family, you'll see."

We walk down a long hallway and into an area that is very much a little girl's room. Laying on the large bed in the middle of the room and sound asleep are Keida and Danny. Raven and the Selin she calls SeeSee lay on the floor at the foot of the bed.

I hear Brittany sigh. "We've tried to separate them. We even made Danny his own room right next door to hers, but nothing has worked. Every evening, I put them both to bed in their own rooms, but in the morning, we always find them this way. Either she's in his room, or he's in hers. I tried to talk to Keida about it, but she says he is hers and she can't sleep without him. She is as stubborn as her dad when her mind is set on something.

And poor Danny has been through so much that I can't make myself scold him. They are just kids, but it doesn't look right. It's crazy how quickly they have become inseparable though, even in their sleep they need to be touching. I had to hold XuL back the first night we found Danny in here with her."

"Of course, he was like *get that boy out of my daughter's bed!* So, I did. I picked Danny up and moved him back only to find that Keida had gone to him sometime in the night. I then proceeded to tell XuL to *go get his daughter out of that boy's bed*, which he didn't like too well, either."

"We don't always understand the needs of another, but since they are little, I don't see the harm. One thing for sure is no one will ever hurt them with these two protectors laying in the room either."

"You aren't wrong there. Raven still doesn't like me touching Danny. She has gotten better about not growling every time one of us walks in the room, but I don't trust her completely."

"Being from such different worlds, do you guys clash often about how to raise and discipline Keida?"

"Discipline? Ha! That little brat gets away with murder, and she will laugh about it as she does it. I'm completely outnumbered when it comes to her, and in the eyes of every male within a mile radius, she can do no wrong.

I have a feeling Danny won't have it that easy though. Being a male, he will be expected to behave a certain way. And since he's not from here, I'm not sure how to prepare him for that. Without changing the subject, are you having the same culture shock I had when I first realized I was on an alien planet?"

"Shock is not a big enough word. At this point, dancing pink elephants could appear and I would be like, ok whatever."

Brittany laughs as she takes my hand. "I'm sure Victoria and Kira are wondering where we are and these two will sleep a while longer.

So, let's go bellyache about the weirdness of this world and then bitch about the things we miss most about Earth."

"That sounds like the most human thing I have heard in forever."

CHAPTER 35
VICTORIA

I walk up to the opening and peak out over the railing. From this point, I feel like I can see almost all of Darverius.

"Vic, you can't fall off love, the balconies on SCOUT have a force-field around them."

I automatically pull the dark shawl I have on up over my head even though I know the sun's rays will no longer hurt me, but old habits are hard to break. As I look out over the skyline, if I didn't know the floor was solid under my feet, I would have sworn I was floating on a cloud.

Strong arms come around me from behind and I feel Ty kiss the top of my head as we simply stand here looking around.

"You know, I thought DaR, and Kira's home was beautiful, but this is a whole other wow factor. It's odd isn't it ... in one world we lived mostly underground and in this world, we're living in a floating city in the sky."

"Would you prefer to live planetside?"

"I don't care where we are as long as we're together, but I will say this place is stunning. It was nice of DaR to let us have it. I think this is the first time in a long time it's just been you and me. I feel like we have always had a houseful. What will we do with all this space all by ourselves?"

"Oh, I believe we can get creative if we put our minds to it. It's been several years since we've had the freedom to christen all the surfaces in the house. And anyway, I believe it was Kira who mentioned that this space was open on SCOUT. This was given to DaR when he first took command and according to SAGE, he never stepped into the place. He has coveted that mountain since he was a youngling. I'm happy to see that he obtained it."

"I will admit that I have enjoyed the conversations I've had with SAGE. Even though she's AI, it's like talking to a real person. Kira was teasing her about SCOUT, saying now that we are living up here, she will get to flirt with him that much more. I thought that was rather cute.

As we were unpacking a few of our belongings we got into a discussion about the differences between our homes on Earth and here. She is very interested in the furniture we had on Earth. She believes there could even be a strong market for them here if advertised properly. Sage asked me if I would help her with some of the designs and to be honest, I'm excited to get started on the project. It will give me something to do while you ... well, you get to become you again here. How is that going anyway? You haven't said much about it."

"I must be scanned by the remaining elite. They want to make sure I have not been reproduced or that I'm not an imposter. Once that is all cleared up, I will have all my belongings that DaR didn't have access to due to the secrecy of some of the documents returned, and then we will take it day by day. I'm in no hurry to return to the position I had before I left. We have enough wealth to enjoy our lives here and I plan on simply doing that for a while."

"I can't believe he kept all your stuff after all these years."

"I will admit I cried like a youngling when I opened that storage chamber and saw everything inside. I should have expected no less from DaR."

A ding sound chimes throughout the room. "Master Tyberius, this is SCOUT, your host for the duration of your stay. I wanted to personally introduce myself and to let you know it is a pleasure to have you both here permanently. Mistress Victoria, I am here at your command. All you have to do is speak my name. Also, I have direct access to SAGE if you need her. Master Tyberius, there is a message incoming; would you like me to connect you at this time?"

"That's fine."

"Ty, can you hear me? I have been trying to get in touch with you for hours now, but that floating knucklehead you're living in wouldn't put me through."

"ANDI?!"

"Who else would it be?"

Ty swings me around in his arms, both of us laughing. "ANDI, it's so good to hear your voice."

"Hey Vic! I'm glad you got the old man there in one piece. You guys have got to come for a flight now. SoL tweaked the Traveler and me a little, and the next thing you know, we are a match made in heaven, or maybe I should say space."

"ANDI, I take it that you and the Traveler are now one?"

"Yes, and I have you to thank for that Ty ... you never gave up on me. And I do want to apologize for putting you guys to sleep on the ship, but no matter the calculations I put in, it was the only way."

"What did I tell you ANDI? It's always easier to ask for forgiveness from the living. Do they already have you on ship rotation?"

"Yes, my first mission is in two cycles. It's a simple tow job, but I'm ready."

"It does my heart good to hear your voice. Don't think that you are going to get out of our late-night conversations just because you're a big shot now."

"It's a date, my friend, until this evening."

I reach my hand up caressing Ty's cheek. "I love to see that smile on your face and while you are in such a good mood, I want to tell you about a conversation. You know all of us girls were together the other day and I heard Katherine say something that's been riding me. How good do you think the boys are at keeping secrets?"

CHAPTER 36

RAZ

The last few risings have taken me away from Katherine for longer than I wanted. So, I'm leaving early, wanting to surprise her. I didn't comm her that I was on my way home. When I land, it takes me a moment to find her. She is sitting behind our home, as she calls it, in the large nest of Ola's, playing with one of the newborn Selin pups.

Ola raises her head up as I come around the corner, a light growl leaving her throat until she sees it's me when I get closer. I run my hand over her head before I step into her nest.

"Hi, you're home early. Have you met our newest member yet? This is Ava. Isn't she beautiful? Will she become a Queen like her mommy?"

"Not all females are Queens, but most of Ola's girls become the head of their packs. That's odd, her markings are different from the others. Normally, they all favor Ola, but she is quite beautiful. The males will be quick to claim her." I no more than say that when I hear Thorn growl. I didn't see him lying on the other side of Katherine.

"Sorry, big guy, I didn't see you there, and it looks like he has already claimed her as his own. That should be interesting. We have a few hours left before darkness settles and I want to show you something." She kisses the pup on the nose and then runs her hand over Ola's head as she walks out of the nest. She brushes off her soft leggings and straightens her shirt before looking up at me.

"Do I need shoes?"

"Nope."

"I didn't figure, since you're so opposed to walking."

I love the way she always laughs when I grab her off the ground and we shoot into the sky. I twirl a few times and she screams out play-fully. As we fly toward my destination, I take the time to circle around the things that Katherine finds interesting. I don't know if I would have adjusted as well to her world as she has to mine.

I see the waterfall I want to show her up ahead and laugh when she points it out to me to take her that way. I fly around the small lake, then through the mist of the waterfall cascading from the rocks above. Making sure no one is around first, I hover about fifteen feet over the water then I ask Katherine,

"Hey, do you know how to swim?"

"Well, yeah why?"

I simply drop her, laughing the whole time as her arms flail around her. Before her body is enveloped by the water, I plunge down, catching her before the top of her head can even get wet.

Her arms immediately grab my shoulders as I tread the water beneath us. Wiping the water from her eyes she hits me playfully on the shoulder. "You ass, that's the last time I ever answer you truthfully. I can't believe I fell for that, but I should have seen it coming."

"I can't believe you fell for that ... literally! But it was fun, wasn't it?"

"Yeah, even if you did give me a partial heart attack."

"I could have flown you around the lake and you might have remembered it if someone mentioned seeing it, but now this will be a fond memory. **You don't always remember the road that got you there, but you always remember the adventures.**"

"I have a feeling that every day will be an adventure with you."

"That's my goal in life, to make you love me like no other before, or after."

"You may want to find another goal since I already do. I love you RaZ. I have from the moment I saw you on the other side of the universe."

"That gives me something to work on then. Since I bypassed my original goal, maybe we can set like a new record of how many orgasms I can give you in one rising."

"Always my prankster."

"I can't help it, I love your smile, I love the way you smell, I love your laughter and the taste of you on my tongue. I can keep going, you know."

"Why don't you get me out of all these wet clothes and show all the ways you can love me instead!"

"I love the way you think!"

EPILOGUE

Katherine

"Ok, my eyes are closed like you told me, but I have had it with all the whispering. Spit it out, what are you all up to?

"We have a surprise for you. Are you willing to play along?"

"You guys have me scared now."

Suddenly I'm surrounded by arms. I seem to be in the middle of a group hug. Even little Keida is hugging my legs, then she tugs on me to come down to her level.

"Come on Aunty Kat, it's a big, big secwet and me hates keeping secwets, so you gots to close your eyes for a looonngg time so I don't gots to keep it anymore."

"Do I still need to keep my eyes closed?"

"Yes, you do," they all say at once. "Now Katherine you know we would never do anything to hurt you, so you are simply going to have to trust us. We are going to wrap a cloth around your eyes so you can't peek. Then you are going to follow our instructions. There are no questions allowed after this blindfold is on."

"Girls, this is creepy as hell, you know that right?" All of them are practically bouncing out of their skin with excitement. "Fine, I will play along."

I feel them tugging at my clothes first, then someone starts filing my nails as another rubs lotion all over me. Then they tug on my hair so much I am convinced I am going to be bald on one side. Then they have me step into a dress of some sort that's so heavy I almost fall backward until Kira grabs my arm.

I have been twisted and pulled from every angle. Even SAGE got in on the act giving instructions toward the end. Finally, I must have passed their inspection because they all get quiet. Then I hear Brit whispering to Alana, "She is gonna knock his socks off."

Kira grabs my hand gently and I turn toward her voice. "Katherine, don't move. We will all be right back. Don't you even try to peek either, do you hear me?"

"Yes, ma'am."

I can hear them all laughing and giggling again. I can't hold back my laughter when Brit yells out that her butt is stuck. This dress is so heavy I almost sit down when I hear SAGE say, "Girls, wrap it up, we're on a timeline, and I believe Kat is getting tired."

Suddenly, they are all yelling instructions again. I hear Brit tell Keida to run and tell her dad that we are on the way. I hear Alana ask about flowers, then about something borrowed. What in the world are these girls up to?

Victoria is suddenly on one side of me, and Kira is on the other. "Ok, one small step at a time, you may want to kick your feet out a little to keep from walking on the material of your dress."

I can't help but joke with them, "All this stuff you guys wrapped around me is a dress? I thought I was going to be a mummy in a sideshow."

There are multiple voices all around us when the girls abruptly let go of me. I feel the cloth being unwrapped from my head and the moment I open my eyes all I can see is myself in a large mirror. A huge looking glass has been placed in the middle of the dark forest. I walk up to the mirror slowly, fighting the tears that have formed in my eyes. I'm wearing my mother's wedding dress. I don't know how... since the dress was lost years ago on Earth. But I'm standing here in awe of its beauty; the long train is fanned out gracefully behind me in yards of detailed lace. The pearls and sequins on the sweetheart neckline sparkle in the glass from the lights hanging in the trees above me. My hair hangs in long curls down my back as a veil hides the top of my face.

Someone hands me a bouquet of flowers seconds before the looking glass is moved out of the way. I gasp at the sight before me. I have no idea who did all of this, but I'm overwhelmed. Strings of lights that look like dancing lightning bugs hang heavily in the trees. A long, carpeted runner has been placed between rows of chairs. But the eye catcher is the massive archway decorated with flowers that is standing alone at the end of it.

And standing in front of it is RaZ. He's all smiles as he looks at my bewildered face. He stands tall in a black vest that shows off the contours of his chest and skintight black pants. His large wings flutter with the excitement that everyone can see clearly on his face. Ty walks up beside me straightening my veil as Victoria moves the flowers around in the bouquet. Victoria kisses me quickly on the cheek. "You are so beautiful", she whispers before she walks around the chairs to take a seat up front.

Ty takes my hand and places it on his arm as I stare at the decorations all around us. It finally dawns on me ... it's a wedding ... and if I'm not mistaken, it's mine!

Ty places his finger under my chin, lifting my eyes up to his. "I may not be your father, Katherine, but you have always felt like a daughter to me. With your permission, Victoria and I would like to give you away in the place of your parents. I believe this wedding is something you have always dreamed of, and I know your mother and father would have wanted this for you."

A sob leaves my throat. I never dreamed in a million years this was what was happening. *How have they kept this from me?*

Ty hands me a handkerchief. "No tears child, hold on to your yesterdays, but remember your heart is ready to take the next steps forward. Now on to your future. Are you ready?"

I wipe my eyes and straighten up. "Wow, ahhh, yes, I believe I am." Soft music flows all around us as Ty leads me forward. RaZ never takes his eyes off me, and I swear I can feel him willing his strength to me as I walk forward. Before I realize it, Ty says something to the crowd that I also didn't notice on the way up here and then I feel the comfort of RaZ's hands in mine.

I stare up at RaZ with my heart on my sleeve. I hear someone say this is an Earthly tradition that the bride and the bride's parents requested. There are sounds everywhere, but it's like I have tunnel vision for RaZ only.

I watch RaZ lift his hand up to silence someone and then he lifts my veil up, taking my cheeks in his hands, gently dropping his lips to mine. I think this the first time I've taken a breath since they took that blindfold off.

"You with me in there, beautiful?"

"RaZ, it's a wedding."

"It's our wedding ... are you happy with your dress?"

"OMG yes, everything is so beautiful!"

"It all dulls in comparison to you. I know I didn't ask you properly and this may be a little late, but will you marry me, Katherine? I mean honestly, I'm not going to let you tell me no now anyway, but I thought that you might appreciate me asking anyway."

He always knows how to break through to me, and I feel myself relax. "Always my prankster. And yes, RaZ, I will marry you. Nothing would make me happier."

RaZ lifts his head from mine and yells out, "Brothers, she said yes!"

I hear laughter all around us and I turn to look at all the people who have made this happen. All the girls have huge smiles on their faces and Kira blows me a kiss while Brit gives me a thumbs up. I have no idea how many of RaZ's brothers are here, but there isn't an empty seat.

Someone clearing their throat behind me has me turning back toward RaZ. I can't hide the smile on my face when I hear him say, "Let's try this again shall we?"

The wedding vows are read, and I say "I Do" with a huge grin on my face. Finally, when DaR pronounces us man and wife, RaZ let out a whoop that makes me jump.

"I've got official paperwork now boys so she is officially off the market!"

He kisses me playfully, then whispers, "Love you."

"Love you more…"

Then we turn to all our loved ones to receive their hugs and well wishes, filling my heart and soul with hope and joy for an unknown future. A bright future with my winged stunt devil. I look up through the trees of the dark forest, gazing up at the night sky just as two shooting stars race across the horizon blinking brightly as they pass overhead. I smile when I realize that was just my dad keeping his promise of walking the stars to always be by my side.

The End

<h1 style="text-align:center">OTHER BOOKS FROM
THIS AUTHOR:</h1>

<u>The Forsaken series</u>

<u>If you want to know more about Tyberius and Victoria here they are!</u>

My Book

<u>Darverius, The House of DaR.</u>

For all my new fans, Tyberius is DaR's father, so the story continues.

My Book

Stand-alone novel

The Playboy and the Waitress

My Book

The Brigands of Ruk

My Book

NOTE FROM THE AUTHOR,

<u>Jennifer Julie Miller:</u>

I hope I have made you laugh, and possibly even squeezed a few tears out of ya. Writing has been a lifelong dream for me, and our dreams are the only thing we have to build on!!!

<u>So GO for it</u>!!!!

Reading is a passion of mine as well. I believe there are Dragons, Unicorns, and multicolored Kitty Cats, because our imaginations are our own uniqueness. I am thankful for the support of my family and friends, even though most think I need to be evaluated.

To my readers, thank you for encouraging me to continue writing even though my worlds and words are a little different.

After all, I'm Appalachian, and I talk Appalachian. Therefore, I write Appalachian. All my books have country girls in them, and that's mainly because I only know how to speak country girl correctly.

Then to the Lord above, whose blessing gave a poor little girl from Ironton a chance to dream!

If you enjoyed this story or any of my others, I ask that you take a few minutes to leave a review on Amazon. It really helps both new and older authors.

If you would like to stay in touch, hear about new releases, give some advice, or just drop a line, my links are below, and I love to talk books.

FOLLOW THE AUTHOR

You can find me on Facebook.

Https://facebook.com/JenniferJulieMiller.

On Twitter.

Https://www.twitter.com/jenniferrick

Or email me at:

Jenniferjuliemiller@gmail.com

Follow me on BookBub.

https://www.bookbub.com/profile/jennifer-julie-miller

Follow me on Amazon.

https://amazon.com/author/jjm5325903

And sign up for my email if you want to learn more about Darverius and DaR's twenty-two ... three ... plus sons.

https://eepurl.com/cfrL8X

www.ingramcontent.com/pod-product-compliance
Lightning Source LLC
Chambersburg PA
CBHW031446160726
47994CB00005B/1893